The Fruitful Pastor

Accomplishing God's objectives for your life
and ministry through consistent growth

Dr. David J. Lunsford

Copyright 2024
David J. Lunsford

All rights reserved. No part of this book may be reproduced or transmitted in any form by any means, electronic or mechanical, including photocopying and recording, or by any information storage and retrieval system, except as may be expressly permitted in writing from the author

ISBN: 9798342807364

Parsonhill
Publishing

This work is lovingly dedicated
to my first wife Sue
who encouraged me in life and ministry,
and in the pursuit of graduate ministry education,
and gave me an excellent example to follow,
as she walked a long, hard path to heaven,

And

To the four congregations who helped me
grow as a believer and pastor,

And

To my second blessing, Darlene,
who has been God's gift
for this era of life and ministry,
and has assisted me greatly
in the writing of this book.

And

Above all, **glory to God** who
"...counted me faithful, putting me into the ministry"

Preface

When I was about 45 years old I completed the requirements for certification by the Association of Certified Biblical Counselors (ACBC). The director at that time asked me to be one of a group of people who would share a testimony of the value of the training at the conference where we would receive our official recognition for completing the program. He explained that he would have people representing different stations in life, a man, a woman, younger, older, etc. "You will represent the middle-aged pastor who is still moving forward."

I asked him if he meant that it was common for pastors my age to be stagnant in their pastoral life. He said "yes" and I believed him as he was in a position to affirm this sad state of affairs as both his previous and current role put him in touch with many pastors over a number of years. I was stunned. If the very nature of the Christian life requires growth, how could a man ignore that mandate? Or, if growing spiritually, how could the leader of a congregation not be zealous to impart his growing spiritual experience to his people and to those who have not yet met the Lord, and to help them do the same with others?

I began to think of how I might address this situation, and the result...many years later, is this book in your hands. Between then and now has been a great deal of education and ministry experience which has only served to increase my burden to help men in ministry grow into all that God has for them.

This book was the final project in my Doctor of Ministry degree. Since completing it I have recently retired from 46 years of vocational ministry. As I approached retirement and in the early days of it, I was frequently asked what I would do now. Simply put, I intend to keep growing in my walk with the Lord and my ability to serve Him in the Church which is His Body. I pray that this work will instruct, encourage, and even provoke you to the same.

CONTENTS

	Preface	7
1	Introduction	12
2	The Call to Ministry	20
	Section One Introduction	38
3	The Mandate of Growth	41
4	The Foundation of Growth	53
5	The Actions of Growth	62
6	The Power of Growth	84
7	The Relationships of Growth	90
8	The Direction of Growth	102
9	The Foundation of Life and Ministry	120
10	Crucial Aspects of Character	136
	Section Two Introduction	159
11	Growing in the Work of a Shepherd	162
12	Growing in the Work of an Overseer	190
13	Under-used Components of Growth	220
	Conclusion	249
	Appendix:	
	A; Guidelines for a Meaningful Meeting with God	253
	B; Baptism Ministry Plan	256
	Bibliography	259

ABBREVIATIONS

NKJV	New King James Version of the Bible
NIV	New International Version of the Bible
KJV	King James Version of the Bible
NASB	New American Standard Version of the Bible
CSB	Christian Standard Version of the Bible
ESV	English Standard Version of the Bible
RSV	Revised Standard Version of the Bible
NT	New Testament

Unless otherwise stated, all Bible portions quoted are from the New King James Version of the Bible.

Chapter 1
INTRODUCTION

"I'm convinced that most pastors are in over their heads." Ralph, a layman in one of the churches I served as a pastor, went on to explain that this was meant as a compliment. He realized that leading a church and trying to help people become disciples of Christ was a challenging, even dangerous, task which he was likening to swimming in the deep end of a pool. Anyone who has been in ministry for more than a short while knows this is true. Generally, men complete a course of education that is meant to prepare them to be undershepherds among Christ's flock and eventually come to their first ministry position full of excitement at the prospect of helping others know the joy and peace of Christ. Then, at some point, reality shows its difficult head. Someone doesn't like the way you sit on the platform, or they are aghast that you wash your car on Sunday afternoon, or your senior pastor expects you to carry out ministry just as he does. People don't like the songs you select or the way you spend your workdays, and your wife believes that she and the children need more of your attention, and that person you have been pouring your life into just rejected Christ and walked away, again.

Serving in a pastoral role is a wonderful calling. Pastors often have the privilege to be present at the new birth of Christians. At times they are invited to enter deeply into the lives of their people and rejoice in their steps of spiritual progress. They have the privilege of "solemnizing" marriages and witnessing the faith of dear saints as they confidently transition to heaven. As years transpire, they have the joy of seeing the cumulative results of ministry, sometimes in generations of believers.

To aspire to the position of a pastor is a good thing, as Paul said in 1 Timothy 3:1. But those who do so often cannot imagine how such a position will bring spiritual, emotional, relational, and even physical demands that will test their walk with the Lord deeply. They do not realize how heavy is the weight of wanting others to know Christ and honor Him in life. They cannot conceive of the pressure created by the competing needs of home and church. They do not understand the burden of leading a group of believers to progress toward Christlikeness. When the hard days come, leaders can be tempted to think they are not suited for the role, or that there is no way to endure, much less enjoy their calling, and that they should seek an exit strategy.

One of the first local church pastors, Timothy, who was discipled by the Apostle Paul, seems to have been in over his head, as indicated by these words of Paul directed toward him personally, "Let no one despise your youth..." (I Timothy 4:12). To another church Paul said, "Now if Timothy comes, see that he may be with you without fear; for he does the work of the Lord, as I also do. Therefore, let no one despise him. But send him on his journey in peace" (1 Corinthians 16:10-11) (emphasis added). Besides the challenges from outsiders, Paul felt the need to urge Timothy to more effective ministry with these instructions: "Consider what I say, and may the Lord give you understanding in all things" (2 Timothy 2:7); and, "Be diligent to present yourself approved to God, a worker who does not need to be ashamed, rightly dividing the word of truth" (2 Timothy 2:15); and regarding his personal walk, "Flee also youthful lusts; but pursue righteousness" (2 Timothy 2:22).

Timothy was an exceptional servant of God as evidenced by Paul's statement, "I have no one like-minded, who will sincerely care for your [the Philippians'] state" (Philippians 2:20). Timothy was more in tune with Paul than any other colleague, yet he struggled with many of the same challenges as today's pastors. Timothy's commission to shepherding by Paul and other spiritual men was not enough to sustain him in ministry—he needed more than that to succeed as a pastor.

In a book full of instructions on how Pastor Timothy was to "conduct himself" (I Timothy 3:15) Paul gave one very broad command, "Stir up the gift of God which is in you through the laying on of my hands" (II Timothy 1:6). The NIV gives the most literal translation of "stir up" as, "fan into flame." Vine comments, "The gift of God is regarded [in this verse] as a fire capable of dying out through neglect." While the gift of pastor-teacher is included in this statement, "The gifts and the calling of God are irrevocable" (Romans 11:29), the effective exercise of it is not automatic, as evidenced by Paul's exhortations to Timothy. Not only is the effectiveness of the pastoral gift not automatic; neither is personal spiritual progress. This is why Paul also exhorted Timothy to, "Meditate on these things; give yourself entirely to them, that your progress may be evident to all" (1 Timothy 4:15). Paul did not give these commands about growth and progress only to his disciples. He applied them to his own life and service in texts like Philippians 3 and 1 Corinthians 9.

Several years ago, for the conclusion of a message, I asked our pianist if I could interview her briefly about learning to play the piano. She readily agreed and suggested she could teach me to play a song in just a few minutes in a technique she used to motivate people to learn to play. After we did that I asked her when she started taking lessons. She replied that she began as a very young girl. "And how long did you take lessons?" I asked. "I'm still taking lessons," she replied (at age 45+)! I was shocked but not surprised to learn that her consistent pursuit of skill was the reason she was/is such an excellent pianist, accompanist, and highly sought-after teacher. The simple yet profound truth for every pastor is this—Paul and Timothy needed to grow, and so do we. Can we ever be so mature, or so skillful, that there is no room for improvement in our life or how we serve the Lord? Pastors must give consistent effort to growth in personal life and in ability to shepherd the flock Christ has entrusted to them. Effective pastoral ministry requires more than a conviction of God's call to pursue the office and the approval of spiritual leaders, it springs from the ground of consistent spiritual growth.

In John 15 we hear Jesus teaching His disciples about spiritual growth when He likens Himself to a vine, what we would this of as the trunk of a tree. He likened believers to the branches on that tree which receive life-giving and growth-enabling nutrients from the trunk. The branch which is connected to the trunk "bears fruit." That is, the branch enlarges and reproduces. God uses the image of a disconnected branch to exhort believers to maintain their connection to Christ. By virtue of our new birth into the family of God, we cannot be disconnected but we can live as though disconnected.[1] That is, we can stifle the development of Christlikeness either by ignorance or by choice. The fruitful pastor is one who abides diligently in Christ, thereby accomplishing God's will in his life and ministry.

This concept of fruitful living and serving should inform our concept of spiritual and pastoral growth AND our concept of personal and vocational success. In discussing the common metrics of church ministry in his excellent book, Center Church, Tim Keller notes two current extreme metrics—one is "success," and the other is "faithfulness." Churches with crowds of people claim that their enlarging numbers demonstrate their effectiveness for Christ. Those congregations with small or decreasing numbers assert that their understanding of and attachment to orthodox biblical truth is true success in Christ.

Christ endorses neither option. Rather He exhorts us to "fruitful" Christian living. According to the Apostle Paul in 1Corinthians 3:5-7, God determines the results of our spiritual

---

[1] This is what Paul communicated in I Corinthians 3:1-4 when he informed the Corinthian church members that they were live *as* carnal (literally "fleshly" meaning as ONLY in the flesh, as an unbeliever would be).

service, while we are responsible for living out His instruction for ministry activity. It is a primary responsibility of the pastor to pay attention to God's truth and make sure he is diligently growing in life and service. The quantity of results (fruit of disciples made and increasing Christlike character) is up to God. It is the pastor's task to do all that he can to lead his flock so they might grow through abiding in Christ, while it is God's role to create the increase. Our self-assessment should not be encouraged by great numbers nor discouraged by the lack. Rather, we should take joy in growth attempted and in the daily victories, the steps toward reproduction, and the visible fruit of new disciples and greater Christlikeness that God will bring in His time and in His way.

In chapter 25 of his gospel, Matthew records a parable in which a man put resources in the hands of his servants and exhorted them to use those resources in such a way as to increase their value. Three different servants were given three different amounts of money. Upon his return, the owner had an accounting and subsequently rewarded two of the servants who gained a profit for him. The third servant was verbally and physically chastised for his failure to use what he was given in such a way as to enlarge it. Three servants were given rewards based on what they did with what they were entrusted. Jesus doesn't expect His servants to make something out of nothing, nor does he expect every servant to accomplish the same quantity of ministry. He only expects us to use what we have in the best way possible for the benefit of His work in the world.

God hasn't dropped us in the deep end of the pool without the ability to swim. He calls men to the wonderful and demanding role of "pastor" but also gives them, "all things that pertain to life and godliness" (II Peter 1:3). He empowers us to grow but requires our effort in the process. While salvation is a free gift from God, spiritual growth comes through the empowerment of the Holy Spirit as we give effort to know and live out God's truth. That is true for every Christian as they pursue the Christ life AND for the leader of a group of Christians that we call a local church.

At 19 years old, when I yielded my life to Christ as a believer, it was out of a frustrating teenage era of life. I can clearly remember the thought, which I believe was from God, urging me to consider devoting my life to helping other Christians not be frustrated as I was. This was my initial "call" to ministry, and it is still a driving burden decades later. I am saddened when I hear of men struggling with life, family, or ministry to the point of throwing in the towel or worse. These failures do not have to happen. God has indeed "given us all things for life and godliness" (2 Peter 1:3), and that includes what we need to lead the flock He has assigned to us to fruitfulness.

If you continue to turn these pages, I will endeavor to enlarge your understanding of how you can grow in life and ministry. We will begin by examining how a man becomes a pastor, then we will follow God's three-fold description of the role of the spiritual leader as the outline of this study. We will consider the quality of being an elder, then the work of caring for the sheep (pastor), and finally the work of leading and managing the local church (bishop). While the men who hold this office can be volunteers (sometimes called "laymen" in the contemporary evangelical world) or paid (vocational) servants of the church, my work is focused on those in vocational ministry.

We will take a fresh look at how spiritual growth happens and why it is important, especially for a pastor. We will look carefully at God's expectation for skill growth which enables a pastor to fulfill Christ's command of fruitful living. I will not define a so-called "perfect" image of what a pastor is to be or do other than the New Testament concept of perfection, which is consistent progress in life and ministry. To that end, our cornerstone will be the plan for spiritual growth written by the Apostle Peter in 2 Peter 1:1-11, then applying that model of growth to our personal life and development as pastors. I will attempt to define God's mandates for pastoral work and give suggestions on how pastors can grow in every area.

One of my adult daughters was eager to introduce me to an associate pastor who preached the Sunday we visited her church. After the introduction, he commented on my having been in ministry for a long time. I said, "Yes, 37 years" (at that time), to which he replied, "Wow, how do you do that?" The work of pastoring often seems as impossible and dangerous as being thrown into the deep end of the pool without knowing how to swim, but serving as a fruitful pastor, long-term, is not a mystery. It happens as we diligently work to grow in our walk with Christ and service to His people.

Chapter 2

THE CALL TO MINISTRY

"Do you hope to be a pastor yourself, someday?" From a different man, this question could have been taken as a backhanded insult, but from this dear older faithful servant of God, I knew he was asking if I expected to move from being an associate pastor of youth and music to being a senior pastor. In his faith circle and generation, there was only one pastor in a church and the "youth guy" wasn't him. I believed his question to be sincere, so I answered him kindly saying that I did expect to become a senior pastor someday.

In my 46 years of vocational ministry, the common understanding of who is a pastor and how a man arrives at that designation has broadened greatly. Beginning in the late 1970's, in the evangelical world, there was a stronger emphasis on the equality among born-again Christians based on the New Testament doctrine that all believers have a spiritual gift from God to participate in the work of Christ. Pastors were taken down off the pedestal of positional recognition and placed on a level playing field with all the saints. An increasing number of churches gradually came to understand that there should normally be more than one elder in a church, usually with some as volunteers and a few as full-time paid workers.

While I appreciate and agree with many of the changes this period brought to the Body of Christ, I suspect that making it easier to become a pastor has contributed to the current phenomenon of more pastors leaving the ministry because of character failure, burnout, frustration, or lack of fruitfulness.

The Barna research group recently released a study in which they said the following:

> **"In 2015, the majority of pastors (63%) were at low risk of burnout, while 26 percent were at medium risk and 11 percent were at high risk.** All told, those are actually pretty positive numbers. Or they were at the time. Since then, the number of pastors at high risk for burnout has nearly **quadrupled to 40 percent**, while the number of pastors at low risk has fallen to 23 percent. **This is a five-alarm fire of a transformation in just a few years' time...**This change is even more pronounced among certain kinds of pastors. For example, while 38 percent of male pastors are considered at high risk for burnout, a full 51 percent of women pastors qualify. And once again, while pastors 45 and older are less likely (36%) to find themselves at high risk for burnout, half (50%) of younger pastors are at high risk."

In short, as some denominations may be seeing an influx of younger pastors or women in leadership, these same groups are getting burned out in their work. If these numbers don't turn around, churches in the future will face a real crisis in leadership as older pastors leave the pulpit with either no replacement or, maybe even worse, a replacement who is already feeling exhausted and considering an exit.[1]

Two of the major sources of difficulty for the pastors who were polled were being, "less confident in their calling today than when they began ministry," and "frequently feeling inadequate for their calling or ministry."[2] Serving the Lord as a shepherd of part of His flock is an extremely challenging endeavor. To do so without the confidence that it is God's will

---

[1] Barna Group. "Why are Pastors Burning out Personally and Collectively." *Barna Access Plus.* March 21, 2023. https://barna.gloo.us/articles/rp-module-1-2.
[2] Ibid.

would make the work seem impossible. The fruitful pastor needs to know why he is in vocational ministry and what that ministry should look like.

The call to vocational ministry

The term "call to ministry" is based in Scripture and spoken of in some circles as a clear absolute when it might be better understood as a useful shorthand that brings together several Biblical concepts. The word "call" in the New Testament is used to refer to God's interaction with believers in reference to several things, including salvation (Romans 8:28-30), marital circumstance (1 Corinthians 7:17), missionary ministry (Acts 13:1-3), righteous living (1 Thessalonians 4:7), apostleship (Romans 1:1) and more. Perhaps the lack of a clear specific use of the term regarding a pastoral call has caused some to devalue or even disbelieve the reality of such a call. While there is not a great deal of Biblical reference to a specific "call" to vocational pastoral ministry, there are several clear principles which should be considered together to constitute the doctrine of call to ministry.

Appointment: God calls leaders

The one consistent theme we see in both the Old and New Testaments, regarding spiritual leaders, is that God calls men to lead His people. The men did not volunteer or apply, they responded to God's invitation, which was not just a request. God called Moses to a leadership role which he tried to refuse, but God was not dissuaded by his excuses. God persisted and Moses relented (Exodus 3). In similar fashion we see God verbally call Samuel and move him through a process that resulted in becoming a key leader of God's people (1 Sam 3, ff.). The closest example to a man volunteering for God's work is recorded in Isaiah 6, yet even in this, we see that Isaiah was brought to a place where he responded to a desperate need expressed by God.

Christ chose the 12 men He would use to begin the Christian era (Mark 3:14, Luke 6:13-16, Matthew 4:18-21). Nowhere is the truth of God's initiation in placing leaders clearer than in these words of Christ about the apostles, "You did not choose Me, but I chose you and appointed you" (John 15:16). We also see the initiating work of God very clearly in Saul's life when Ananias was sent to, "Go [help Saul], for he is a chosen vessel of Mine to bear My name before Gentiles, kings, and the children of Israel" (Acts 9:15).

We read of a further work of God later in the life of Saul, who became Paul, to call him into ministry. "Now in the church that was at Antioch there were certain prophets and teachers: Barnabas, Simeon who was called Niger, Lucius of Cyrene, Manaen who had been brought up with Herod the tetrarch, and Saul. As they ministered to the Lord and fasted, the Holy Spirit said, 'Now separate to Me Barnabas and Saul for the work to which I have called them'" (Acts 13:1-2). God moved through the local assembly of believers to bring men into leadership.

A most significant part of God's initiating work in placing spiritual leaders in the Body of Christ is by endowing believers with special abilities for service. God gives each believer one or more spiritual gifts (1 Corinthians 12:7, Romans 12:6). These supernatural abilities to serve the Body of Christ include teaching (I Corinthians 12:28) and pastor/teacher (Ephesians 4:11). God sovereignly chooses to whom He will give the various gifts necessary for the functioning of the church (1 Corinthians 12:11). A man cannot succeed in the role of pastor without the appropriate spiritual gift. Spiritual leadership isn't a job, even if it comes with a paycheck. Rather, it is a divine trust from God.

The call of God to spiritual leadership is strongly affirmed by these words of Paul to the pastors at Ephesus, "Therefore take heed to yourselves and to all the flock, among which the Holy Spirit has made you overseers, to shepherd the church of God which He purchased with His own blood" (Acts

20:28). It is noteworthy that we do not know the exact process by which these elders entered their role, "The Holy Ghost made, literally, placed or set, not only by creating the office, but by choosing the incumbents, either by express designation (as in Acts 13:2) or by directing the choice of others (as in 6:5)."[3] Even though we read that Paul, "appointed elders in every church" (Acts 14:23), and that Titus was likewise commanded to appoint elders (Titus 1:5), we understand God was the force in the process. Dave Hegg summarizes this truth well: "God drafts those he intends to use in leadership."[4]

Aspiration: men perceive the call

It is worth noting that many men whom God has called to His service were taken by surprise. Moses was flabbergasted to think that God wanted him to give a message to the Pharoah. Samuel had no clue who was talking to him. Gideon was terrified of God's request. Paul was going in the exact opposite direction of God's desire for his life. From what we read of Timothy; he doesn't sound like someone who volunteered for spiritual leadership. The principle here is that the men God calls are not those who see themselves as something special with extraordinary abilities (1 Corinthians 1:26-31). Many effective pastors I know personally, who have pastored well, have similar stories; this author included. Rather than chasing after the pastorate, I ran from it until I could no longer resist God's conviction.

Even though God does the choosing and empowering, men eventually perceive His call in the form of a desire for the position (1 Timothy 3:1). The **KJV** and the **NKJV** miss something that the **NIV** and **NASB** include in their translations of this seminal verse. There are two different words translated

---

[3]Alexander, Joseph Addison. *A Commentary on the Acts of the Apostles.* Liverpool, UK: Banner of Truth Trust, 1857, 249.
[4]Hegg, David W. *Appointed to Preach.* Fearn, Ross-shire, Great Britain: Christian Focus Publications, 1999, 17.

"desire." The first is, "to stretch oneself out in order to touch or grasp something, to reach after or desire something."[5] The other word is the more common word for desire defined as, "desire, craving, or longing."[6] The NIV captures this when it says, "If any man **aspires** to the office of overseer, it is a fine work he **desires** to do." I very much appreciate the thought expressed by Jamieson in his work on how men become pastors where he titles his first chapter, "Say 'I Aspire,' Not 'I'm Called'."[7] He goes on to say that there is a difference between claiming to know God's mind ("He has called me") and expressing a sincere desire ("I think He is leading me to this work which I want to do"). In describing the "desire" of 1 Timothy 3:1 Allen puts it well, "This word refers to the inward compulsion, or passion, for ministry. It is what's taking place in your inner person that leads you to 'aspire,' or pursue practically, ministerial service. These two words—aspire and desire—must go together. If you desire the ministry, you will aspire to it."[8]

    The net effect of God's call and a man's desire to answer that call is that he becomes "eager" (I Peter 5:2) to do the work of a shepherd. Such a man does not pursue the office of overseer by some outward compulsion or sinful inner drive. He is "volunteering" (1 Peter 5:2 NASB), that is, he is "willingly" (1 Peter 5:2 NIV, NKJV) going after the work. I believe this is what some Christians mean when they say they "surrendered" for ministry. I would certainly use that word in my case as I was running from God's call until I was compelled to make myself a living sacrifice (Romans 12:1). In my devotion to Christ, I

---

[5]Thayer, Joseph Henry. *Thayer's Greek English Lexicon of the New Testatment.* Grand Rapids, Michigan: Zondervan, 1974, 452.
[6]Thayer, Joseph Henry. *Thayer's Greek English Lexicon of the New Testatment.* Grand Rapids, Michigan: Zondervan, 1974, 238.
[7]Jamieson, Bobby. *The Path to Being a Pastor.* Wheaton, IL: Crossway, 2021, 19.
[8]Allen, Jason K. *Discerning Your Call To Ministry.* Chicago, IL: Moody Publishers, 2016, 29.

became a willing worker for what I discovered was His call to ministry.

I have known several men in the churches I served who were definitely elders in life and ability. One of them said two things to me that gave me pause. First, he said, "If you ever need someone to fill the pulpit, I'd be happy to do so." This was a welcome offer in a church where I was the solo pastor and our budget for guests was limited. He had taught Sunday school, and I knew he was capable with the Word. The second statement stuck in my mind as I was in the early days of evaluating eldership, "I'd never want to have your job." This wasn't the only man I had known over the years who had the character of an elder, was seen as a spiritual leader in the church, was capable to teach the Word, yet did not want to be a vocational senior pastor. I worked with a seminary graduate who had a sincere desire to do a certain ministry, which our church felt was a perfect fit. After doing part-time ministry for a few months, he quit and never entered vocational ministry. If a man is called and gifted by God to be a pastor, he will aspire to and desire that office. Without that driving desire, he will not be one of Christ's under-shepherds.

There is, however, a danger inherent in the pursuit of the pastorate, which is wanting the position rather than wanting to do the work God intends for that position. The office of spiritual leadership should be sought because a man wants to help others know Christ and grow up in Him. Derek Prime says it well in his work on pastoring, "The call usually begins with a desire to care for the spiritual well-being of others and to preach God's Word."[9] The burden God laid on my heart was to help others avoid the spiritual frustration I had experienced as an ungodly Christian teenager. After several more years of preparation, I was given that very opportunity.

---

[9]Prime & Begg. *On Being a Pastor.* Chicago: Moody, 2004, 22.

Appreciation: the Body of Christ observes the call

In the Church era in which we live, God works through the Body of Christ as expressed in local assemblies of Christians. The New Testament is rife with examples of how God worked through various local churches, including using the Body of Christ to identify men for pastoral ministry. Paul was first welcomed and recognized as a spiritual leader by a local church in Damascus, then by the Jerusalem church (Acts 9:10-43). Timothy was declared to be a pastor "with the laying on of the hands of the eldership" (1 Timothy 4:14). Timothy was instructed, "Do not lay hands on anyone hastily," indicating that the task of finding spiritual leaders was part of his work as the pastor of a local church (1 Timothy 5:22). Derek Prime captures the truth well even though he uses an unfamiliar (to me) term, "It has been traditional to speak of the double call to the ministry: There is first the inward call an individual becomes personally aware of; there is, second the outward call of God's people as they recognize the calling and gifts an individual has for the ministry."[10]

A most significant part of validating the call of God on an individual is the work of the congregation in recognizing the fitness of a man for pastoral ministry. The qualifications for spiritual leaders listed in 1 Timothy 3:1-7 and Titus 1:5-9 are qualities that can only be seen in the context of the local church. A man alone in a room may believe he has all the goodness of Christ, but in the crucible of local church ministry, his real character and ability are revealed. Some might argue that these instructions were only for Timothy and Titus to use in their selection of elders, as though their time frame was unique to the first-generation church and hence doesn't apply to us today. Even they could not evaluate a man for ministry without seeing him in action.

---

[10]Prime, Begg &. *On Being a Pastor.* Chicago: Moody, 2004, 24.

Affirmation: The Body of Christ acknowledges the call

The combination of the call of God and the demonstration of qualification by a man in a local church leads to the affirmation of that man's call to pastoral ministry. Such was the case in the life of Paul seen when we combine Romans 1:1, "Paul, a bondservant of Jesus Christ, called to be an apostle, separated to the gospel of God," and Acts 13:2, "As they ministered to the Lord [in the local church] and fasted, the Holy Spirit said, 'Now separate to Me Barnabas and Saul for the work to which I have called them.'" God called Paul and the church recognized that call. (It would be ludicrous to imagine the church sending Paul as a missionary ONLY because the Holy Spirit said so, even though they did not affirm his life and gifting!) This recognition began shortly after Paul was born again; "Immediately **he preached** the Christ in the synagogues, that He is the Son of God. Then all who heard were **amazed**, and said, 'Is this not he who destroyed those who called on this name in Jerusalem, and has come here for that purpose, so that he might bring them bound to the chief priests?' But Saul **increased** all the more in strength, and confounded the Jews who dwelt in Damascus, proving that this Jesus is the Christ" (Acts 9:20-22).

I'm sure Paul was a hot topic of discussion in the Damascus church and everywhere he went, especially in the early days after his conversion. Eventually, all the Christians (other than the haters!) recognized what God had done in him. I had an epiphany in a class some years ago as the teacher asserted that the way we perceive our spiritual gift is by what we gravitate toward in the Body of Christ. His understanding was that a person's gift works, or is active, if they are walking in Christ. They don't need to take a gift inventory; they need to follow the prompting of the Holy Spirit. As I evaluated my ministry, I realized that my gift of teaching or pastor/teacher is what I use to do ministry whether in the pulpit or the board meeting or counseling room. I just "naturally" explain things spiritually, and God works through it.

When I first put myself on the altar of living sacrifice and began to aspire to the pastorate, God made that call operative, even though I didn't recognize it at the time. For a reason I cannot remember, I instituted an "open door" policy in my Bible College dorm room and welcomed fellow students (only men!) into my room any time the door was open. Several men came regularly for what we would now call "mentoring." A year later I was given a significant leadership position by the school which I didn't ask for. I took it, assuming I was up to it, since they asked, and thoroughly enjoyed the ministry. In retrospect, I'm not sure if I would even consider giving such a responsibility to a 20-year-old. I believe that God was at work in me to empower me for that (sort-of pastoral) role even beyond my awareness at the time.

The most important affirmation of the call to spiritual leadership is this—if God has called a man to be a pastor, when that man does the pastoral ministry it is effective. When he teaches, people learn. When he counsels, people change. When he visits, people are encouraged. When he leads, progress is made. This impact will happen because he is living out the spiritual gift(s) God has placed in him. I understand that leading God's sheep comes with challenges and difficulty, but I am speaking broadly of the impact of a man genuinely called by God. Recently, I ran into a man who was a teen in my youth ministry. He expressed a deep appreciation for how I helped him at a time when he was struggling in His walk with the Lord. Over the years he solidified as a Christ-follower and has now walked that path for decades. I was unaware of his struggles at the time, but God used the ministry I did (quite feebly I often thought in those years) to reach this young man. That kind of fruit indicates that God is indeed at work through those He calls into His service.

Ultimately, the affirmation of the body of Christ finds its apex in one or more things. Ordination is a key expression of affirmation and usually comes within a few years of a man's first ministry after he has proven himself in the role. Those churches or schools which ordain men who have not proven themselves do great potential harm to the man and the church. The positive evaluation by fellow pastors and the agreement of a congregation who has observed a man in action over time is a key affirmation of God's call. The other key affirmation is a call by a church to become their pastor after a rigorous evaluation process.

Jim Vogel expresses the interplay of personal desire and affirmation by the congregation when he says, "These Biblical requirements and spiritual observations cooperate as a unified entity and may both privately (within the heart of the one called) and publicly (within the body of the local church) demonstrate the call of God's Spirit upon a man for vocational ministry...both parts need to be 'syncretistically' viewed by the reader. What I mean by this is that each part works in harmony with the other and that within each part there is mutual dependence. So, failure in one requirement will obstruct the whole."[11] A man who desires to be a pastor must be observed and then (when appropriate) affirmed by the Body of Christ in his aspiration.

What does God call men to?

"What do you do all week?" is a question I have been asked many times by people inside and outside the church, often with a twinkle in their eye. I love to respond to their jest with one of my own, "I work one hour a week, and it takes four men to collect the offering!" This question is sometimes asked to poke fun at the guy who seems to have an easy job, and other times people are genuinely curious to know how the designated key spiritual leader of a church spends his work week. It is a legitimate question, especially when asked by those less familiar with God's plan for the Body of Christ and its leaders. The concise answer which I would give after many years of living it

---

[11] Vogel, Jim. *The Pastor, A Guide for God's Faithful Servant.* Arlington Heights, IL: Regular Baptist Press, 2012, 22.

out is this; I try to live out the job description God has given me as a shepherd of His sheep.

The New Testament uses three words to refer to the role of spiritual leadership and the men who occupy that role: elder, bishop, and pastor. A better translation of 1 Timothy 3:1 would speak of a man who aspires "to be a bishop." The word "office" (KJV) or "position" (NKJV) is supplied to smooth the translation. The desire expressed is to be an overseer, that is, a leader in the local church. In the New Testament this role is more often referred to as that of an "elder." The work done by the *elder/overseer* is that of a *shepherd* which is translated "pastor" in Ephesians 4:11. 1 Peter 5:1-4 uses all three words to refer to the men who hold the role when it addresses the "elders," and exhorts them to "shepherd" (pastor) the flock, and to "oversee" (bishop) those God has assigned to them.

The interplay of these words in the New Testament is vitally important for those who aspire to the role of local church pastor. A man cannot pick and choose among the roles according to his preference. The list of qualifications for the overseer in 1 Timothy 3 makes it clear that the leader must be spiritually mature. Usually, a newer Christian has not become "blameless" in all the qualities Paul listed. Only growth over time can bring a man to spiritual maturity. This is inherent in the term **"elder."** The position of spiritual leadership should spring out from a man's experience of walking with the Lord. Shepherding God's people is about helping them walk with Christ, not about holding a position or being known as someone important in a certain circle. This is the danger of the pastorate which was expressed in 1 Timothy 3:6, "He must not be a recent convert, or he may become conceited and fall under the same judgment as the devil" (NIV). No amount of zeal to do the Lord's work as a pastor can take the place of spiritual maturity.

The word **"overseer"** expresses the leadership aspect of the role of a pastor. Every Christian has a gift which contributes to the function of the local church, but leadership and management are still required. God wants things done "decently and in order" (1 Corinthians 14:40) and that only happens with supervision. We will examine this aspect of ministry in depth later, but this is part of what God calls a man to do in the pastorate. Many men are happy to say they are called to teach and preach yet find the work of management to be difficult and they essentially refuse or are scared to lead. I heard a deacon in a local church quote a previous pastor as saying, "Leading the church is your [deacons] job." No, it is the job of the elder(s). If you aspire to be a pastor, you will desire to lead the local church.

The third, and in many ways, most familiar word about the role of spiritual leadership is "**pastor**." This is the least used of the three terms in the New Testament and is a translation of a Greek word that means, "shepherd."[12] We will also take a more in-depth look at this aspect of spiritual leadership later, but for now, I would have you realize that caring for God's people is a (the?) key descriptor of the role of spiritual leader. Shepherding begins with teaching but is more than standing up front on Sunday mornings. Shepherding includes all aspects of helping people walk with Christ and often needs to be done up close and in person. If you aspire to be a recognized leader in a church, you are aspiring to care for God's sheep (Acts 20:28).

I disagree somewhat with Jason Allen when he writes, "The call to ministry is essentially a call to the ministry of the Word. Stated another way, a call to preach or teach the Word is the distinguishing mark of a call to the ministry."[13] I say "somewhat" because this idea is what drives some men to believe they are called *only* to teach, not to the complete work of spiritual leadership in the local church. The call of God is to be

---

[12]*The New International Dictionary of New Testatment Theology Volume 3.* Edited by Colin Brown. Grand Rapids, MI: Zondervan, 1978, 564.
[13]Allen, Jason K. *Discerning Your Call To Ministry.* Chicago, IL: Moody Publishers, 2016, 22.

an example (**elder**), to guide the ministry of the saints to one another (**bishop**), through the teaching of the Word of God (**pastor**) in public, in private, and in leadership settings. Sometimes this looks like a discussion over lunch with a hurting father, sometimes like pulpit oration, and sometimes like a leadership planning meeting.

The call to ministry is foundational

As a police and fire department chaplain, I was invited to participate in a major disaster drill at a nearby international airport. My task was to get inside the controlled perimeter without prior approval or official connection to any responding unit. I showed my local department badge and kept saying I was with them and before long, I was in, and everyone believed I belonged. It is possible to get into ministry in like fashion, that is, just by personal persistent initiative. But that kind of entrance to the pastorate will not result in genuine fruitfulness, and eventually such a man may walk away because God is not holding him in and up.

Entering ministry the right way requires patience. God frequently has a different timetable than we do. It isn't hard for a man to "make" church activity happen, but real character and fruitful ministry can only be discerned over time within the context of the body of Christ. I had a good friend in college who believed he was called to be a pastor. After a couple of years of schooling, he was married to a lovely woman he met on campus. For the next several years he had a series of excellent jobs and eventually finished school and entered vocational ministry—after his wife agreed from her heart with his desire. He went on to be a very fruitful pastor and Bible College teacher. God's timing is not always what we envision. If you have genuinely been called of God, or even if you are not quite certain but hope you are, find a godly mentor—preferably your pastor—and follow his guidance as you work toward affirmation by the body of Christ.

The call to ministry is not enough

Timothy was gifted for pastoral ministry (1 Timothy 4:14) but he still needed to nurture that gift. A few years after Paul commented on Timothy's gifting, he wrote this, "Therefore I remind you to stir up the gift of God which is in you through the laying on of my hands" (1 Timothy 1:6). In the following verses (the whole book?) he instructs Timothy on how to stir up the gift. That is what the rest of this work is about, developing your life and ministry in the Lord day by day for all the years God will give you. Praise God for His work in your life but realize that even with His empowerment for ministry, you will only be genuinely fruitful as you grow in life and pastoral skill.

We will consider this needed growth by first understanding how spiritual growth happens. Peter has given us a clear "how-to" explanation of growing in Christ. We will consider how to put that plan of growth into practice by looking at the three aspects of pastoral ministry: elder, bishop, pastor.

IDEAS/QUESTIONS FOR APPLICATION

Write out your call to the pastorate

- If you are an aspiring pastor, do your best to summarize why you want to be a pastor and what were the circumstances in which you felt the draw of God toward pastoral ministry.

- If you are a seasoned servant and have never written an account of the call of God, do it now and ask God to help you see how He called you. If you have written this out previously, revisit it and evaluate what you wrote and add to it or edit it as you now see God's work in your life.

Evaluate your qualification for ministry

- Create a meditation/memory card for 1 Timothy 3:1-7. Create a plan for reading and meditating on this passage ("think on these things"). If you have not done so previously, study the words so that you have a clear understanding of their meaning then use those definitions to evaluate your life.

- If you are an aspiring pastor, ask several people such as your wife (if you have one, or your fiancée' if you have one), trusted friends, coworkers, and your pastor to give you feedback on how your life matches the qualifications.

- If you are seasoned pastor who genuinely wants to grow, ask some of the same people listed above to evaluate you. Listen to their evaluations (I will speak about having a "listening ear" in the coming chapters).

Assess your pastoral readiness

- If you are an aspiring pastor, evaluate how ready you are for a pastoral role. Prayerfully consider (in conjunction with the input you received from others) what further preparation, mentoring, or experience might help you be more fully prepared. Keep these areas of needed growth in mind as you consider personal and pastoral growth in the rest of this book.

- If you are a seasoned pastor, evaluate your life and ministry and choose some targets for growth in light of 1 Timothy 3. Keep these in mind as you read the next few chapters which are focused in detail on how to grow in Christ.

Introduction to section 1

GROWING AS AN ELDER

There are three terms in the New Testament that refer to the office often called the "pastorate" by many in the modern Evangelical world. The word "elder" is used 23 times from the book of Acts to the book of 1 Peter to describe the men who were recognized leaders in local churches. The term, "pastor," is only used twice in the New Testament and the word "bishop" (KJV, NKJV) or "overseer" (NIV, NASB) is used five times to identify the role of spiritual leader and one time to identify the work of leadership. The use of all three terms together in Acts 20:17, 28 and I Peter 5:1-2 makes it clear that they all refer to the same office. It would be appropriate to call a man in vocational ministry by any of the three terms.

The word elder literally means to "be older" (C. Brown, TNIDT 1975). As a term it came to signify, "more honored...In the order of society, the elders receive respect and authority on the ground of their experience and wisdom."[1] A form of the word is translated "ambassador" in 2 Corinthians 5:20 and Ephesians 6:20 (KJV, NKJV, NIV, NASB, ESV). The civil leaders of the Jews in the time of Christ were called "elders." From the various uses we understand that the word conveys leadership based in maturity.

The concept of maturity is broad and deep in the New Testament. In Philippians 3 the Apostle Paul defined mature Christians both as those who are consistently growing toward

---

[1]Brown, Colin. *The New International Dictionary of New Testament Theology.* Edited by Colin Brown. Vol. 1. Grand Rapids, MI: Zondervan, 1975, 188.

Christlike perfection (Philippians 3:9-11) AND those who are relatively mature compared to other Christians (Philippians 3:15-16). This is the sense in which the word "elder" is used of those in spiritual leadership. It is not as I heard from a deacon in a church that was of a certain cultural background that recognizes age above all, "The older people with money are the elders in our church, both men and women."[2]

    The maturity which makes one an elder in a local body of Christ is defined by the requirements of the role in 1 Timothy 3 and Titus 1. To be an elder is to be *recognizably* mature in Christ, enough that church members readily identify such men as worthy of the role of leadership. While only those men who are called by God can genuinely function in the role of elder, the path to that position for those who desire it requires spiritual growth as does the execution of that role. Thus, my primary focus for those who desire the office of an elder, or who already possess it, is on spiritual growth. The next several chapters will explain how we grow in Christ. After that we will turn to more specific issues which must be addressed by the man who would be a fruitful spiritual leader.

---

[2] This is a firsthand report from a man who was helping to bring about change in the churches of a certain ethnic people group. He brought a congregation to use our facility for a time.

Chapter 3

THE MANDATE OF GROWTH

MANY years ago, I pushed "Play" on a cassette player with a tape from the first session of a conference for pastors put on by Jerry Falwell. Someone had given me the recordings, so I thought I should at least return the favor with a courtesy listen. I was both pleasantly surprised and a bit shocked to hear the first thing Jerry Falwell said to a room full of pastors. He exhorted them to spend time in the Word and in prayer every day just for themselves. I was taken aback that such an exhortation would be needed for that audience. Doesn't it go without saying that of all Christians, those who are spiritual leaders would be spending time in the Word and prayer so they might grow in Christ? Yet, the rate of burn-out, drop-out, fail-out, and even suicide by men in ministry makes one wonder if some of those who have dedicated themselves to serve God may not be taking seriously the need of spiritual growth which they so ardently promote to others.

Spiritual growth is commanded by Christ

The mandate of spiritual growth for the Christian begins with the first recorded major public teaching of Jesus Christ. In Matthew 5:6 He said, "Blessed are those who hunger and thirst for righteousness." This leaves little room for a stagnant Christian life or the assumption that one can reach such a pinnacle of maturity that growth is no longer needed. Christ intends for his disciples to be consistently reaching forward to put on more of the righteous character He has made available to them.

In Matthew 5:20 Jesus taught that God-pleasing righteousness goes beyond mere external appearance. The external can be put on much easier than true internal change that leads to a visible transformation which is only obtained by those who are consistently working toward it. The path to this internal change is spoken by Christ in Matthew 7:24-27, where Jesus exhorted His listeners to "do" His teachings—that is, to apply them in their life. *Knowledge* of the truth is not the goal, *life change* is.

This life change is described by Jesus in John 15:1-8 in which He makes the expectation for His followers unavoidably clear. Those who claim to follow Christ must bear fruit—that is, they must be growing according to normal expectations. A healthy fruit tree normally enlarges and reproduces consistently year by year. Christ chose that object lesson to summarize the mandate for His disciples. A tree that stops growing and bearing fruit is not viewed as a kind of ultra-mature tree just because it has been alive for many years and has borne fruit in the past. Likewise, the Christian of many years, whose growth was paused long ago, is not pleasing Christ, and should not be viewed as a spiritual leader simply because of many years in Christ and the fruit once born.

Spiritual growth is God's plan for the Christian life

One of the seminal passages on spiritual growth is Romans 6 in which Paul enunciates the wonderful truth that believers have been freed from the power of sin (vv. 1-6) and infused with the life of Christ which empowers righteous living (vv.7-10). The opening statement in this passage makes it clear that living in sin is not an option for the believer; "Shall we continue in sin...certainly not!" Likewise, the commands in vv. 11-13 push believers to grow out of sin and into righteousness.

Another foundational passage in the understanding of Christian growth is Ephesians 4:17-24. There believers are instructed to stop acting like unbelievers and start acting like born-again Christ-followers. This is done through the *purposeful* putting off of sin in thought and deed and the putting on of righteous thoughts and actions.

The apex in our understanding of the necessity for consistent spiritual growth comes in the form of a personal testimony of the Apostle Paul in Philippians 3:8-11. Paul states that his life's goal was to become like Christ, which, to that point he had not yet accomplished, but on which he was focused in a life-long pursuit. In no way does he believe he has arrived at the end of that journey; rather, he sees his need for a constant effort in acquiring more Christ-like character.

Spiritual growth is especially important for the Pastor

Beyond the normal expectations of spiritual growth for all believers, the man who holds the position of spiritual leadership within the Body of Christ has greater expectations from God. The Apostle Paul penned the books we call the "pastoral epistles" which were revealed by God through the real-life ministries of two specific men who were leaders of local churches. In I Timothy 4:12 Paul told pastor Timothy to defeat criticism with exemplary conduct. One is not characterized by exemplary conduct without consistent growth. A pastor cannot be known, as was the employee of a friend of mine; "He said he had 10 years of experience, but the truth is he had one year of experience and repeated it 10 times." No matter how much a pastor has grown, there is always more progress to be made if he would be a model for believers as Paul exhorted and embodied in I Corinthians 11:1.

1 Timothy 4:15 contains a command for Timothy to meditate on Paul's instructions and to "give himself" to them. This strongly implies that Timothy would need to prayerfully consider the importance of the instructions and work at making them part of his life. Such thought and action do not come without effort. 1 Timothy 6:11-14 contains a series of commands: **flee** covetousness, **pursue** righteousness, **fight** the

good fight of faith, and **hold on** to eternal life. Each of these commands implies that the godly and effective pastoral life can only be possessed with purposeful effort. 2 Timothy 2:15 continues in this same vein with the instruction to be **diligent** to be skilled in using God's Word. The imagery in this verse comes from a word that means to "cut a straight line,"[3] as with a piece of wood or other material. The implication is that a tradesman would be considered a craftsman if he were able to cut a straight line (in that day of rudimentary tools). One only becomes a craftsman with instruction, practice, and coaching from a mentor. This doesn't happen automatically, accidentally, or haphazardly.

    2 Timothy 3:17 contains a declaration that mandates spiritual growth in the believer and pastor above all the other instructions when it says that the purpose of the Word of God is to make Christ-followers "perfect" (KJV) or "complete" (NKJV) or "thoroughly equipped" (NIV). All these translations fall a bit short of the original Greek, which uses the same root word twice in one sentence to emphasize the extent to which the Word of God enables spiritual maturity. A more literal translation would say that the Word of God enables a believer to be "fitted" or "equipped" for every good work by virtue of having been "super equipped" or "thoroughly equipped." The point we must grasp is that because we have been endowed with the nature of Christ, God's Word is able to transform our lives so that we can do all the works God calls us to do. This whole life transformation comes only by a life of *effort* to *grow* in Christ.

    Pastors also have a unique reason to grow in Christ which is recorded in 1 Timothy 4:16, "Take heed to yourself and to the doctrine. Continue in them, for in doing this you will save both yourself and those who hear you." Paul exhorts Timothy to be certain of the truth he lives by and teaches

---

[3]Brown, Colin. *The New International Dictionary of New Testament Theology.* Edited by Colin Brown. Vol. 3. Grand Rapids, MI: Zondervan, 1978, 352.

BECAUSE so much hangs in the balance. We understand that pastors don't "save" anyone on their own initiative or by their own strength or skill. However, we do know that God in His sovereignty uses frail human shepherds to enunciate His truth. If the truth is unclear or wrongly taught or poorly communicated, the result in lives can be ruinous, starting with his own.

The essence of spiritual leadership begins with the pastor's own life and his own home where he is to love his wife as Christ loved the church and with her rear children who walk in the Lord. The pastor who is not diligent to grow in the knowledge and application of the Word will engender weak, immature, struggling Christians in the church and will contribute to the breakdown of his own family. A stagnant pastor cannot *stop* the spiritual growth of his church members, but if he is their main source of spiritual input, his lack of growth will likely be reflected in theirs. A flock that does not reproduce is a dying flock. Not only does a shepherd's lack of growth affect his flock's spiritual maturing, but his vision and management of the church will spring from human wisdom, not godly. The result will be a body of believers which is not living in Christlike character.

Spiritual growth is irreplaceable
A spiritually productive life

In the opening chapter of Peter's final message, he relays the divine perspective on the value of spiritual growth, "For if these things *[the spiritual growth explained in vs. 1-7]* are yours and abound, you will be neither barren nor unfruitful in the knowledge of our Lord Jesus Christ" (2 Peter 1:8). The result of Christian growth is stated in a negative way that yields a positive result. The word "barren" literally means "inactive, idle...lazy, shunning the labor which one ought to perform."[4] The NIV seems to convey the fuller idea with its use of "ineffective." God saved us for a purpose. "We are His workmanship, created in Christ Jesus for good works" (Ephesians 2:10). If believers are not growing in Christ, they will not accomplish that for which God saved them. They will be like a fellow I worked with in a temporary job during college years who told me that the goal was to work as slow as possible to get more pay. I suspect that his father, the man who hired us, would not have agreed.

The word "unfruitful" means just that. It is used literally in the Scripture (as in Matthew 7:17) and figuratively, as it is here. It takes us back to the words of Christ in John 15:5, "I am the vine, you are the branches; he who abides in Me and I in him, bears much fruit, for apart from Me you can do nothing." We are connected to Christ organically. We have His power running through our veins. We can become like Him—if we diligently work at it. When we do nothing, we are unfruitful; that is, unproductive in the very things He most desires from us. To give little or less than diligent effort to growing in Christ is to waste our opportunity and disappoint our Savior.

Rather than striving to make oneself significant by pastoring a large church through whatever human methods he might employ, the godly pastor can rest in God's single expectation of him—fruitful spiritual growth. Perhaps God's plan for your life is to lead a megachurch or perhaps it will be somewhere that seems less significant. The wonderful potential for all men of God is that they will please God and accomplish HIS will if they are consistently growing in life and ministry ability.

---

[4]Thayer, Joseph Henry. *Thayer's Greek English Lexicon of the New Testatment.* Grand Rapids, Michigan: Zondervan, 1974, 72.

A spiritually victorious life

According to 2 Peter 1:9, the failure to grow arises from a sort of divine dementia in which the believer has forgotten that he was saved and empowered to conquer sin and live like Christ. Such forgetfulness could only come from a prolonged period of ignoring one's life in Christ. God expects His children to use what He has given to them. His call to growth means that the lack of growth is itself a sin. The constant stream of choices we must make each day about right and wrong also means that the absence of forward motion equals regression. Taken together with the instruction in verse eight, the faithful believer-pastor should realize that he can be productive in Christ, and he must not waste his days in stagnation, which is actually sinful living, with nothing to show for it. No matter what the life circumstances, every day can be eternally meaningful if the believer is growing in Christ.

A spiritually safe life

Peter makes two astounding claims in 2 Peter 1:10, "Therefore, brethren, be even more diligent to make your call and election sure, for if you do these things, you will never stumble." The process of Christian growth results in two aspects of spiritual safety. The first is the assurance of salvation, that is, we can "make our call and election sure." The Apostle John penned words that define the key evidence of a genuine spiritual life, "If we say that we have fellowship with Him, and walk in darkness, we lie and do not practice the truth. But if we walk in the light as He is in the light, we have fellowship with one another, and the blood of Jesus Christ His Son cleanses us from all sin" (1 John 1:6-7). The way to consistently "walk in the light" is to be growing in Christ. The stagnant believer isn't standing still but is becoming spiritually foul like a standing body of water. When a believer is growing in Christ, they have an awareness of the presence of God and the evidence of an increasing

Christlikeness in thought and deed, thereby walking confidently in the divine relationship created by the Holy Spirit.

The second promise of safety in II Peter 1:10 is protection from unseen dangers. When we are diligent to grow in Christ, we gain strength and dexterity which enables us to avoid spiritual trip-and-fall hazards which Peter calls "stumbling." When we get out of bed in the middle of the night, we are susceptible to "tripping" over things we cannot see. The solution is to turn on the light and walk confidently around and over the obstacles. In a similar fashion, the Christian who is growing day by day gains God's ability to see and avoid or properly handle dangers that fall into his path.

How ironic that God would use a serial failure like Peter to exhort all future believers on how to avoid stumbling! Peter knew what it was to trip over spiritual hazards, but he came to know what it was like to walk confidently and carefully through incredible challenges. A believer can be prepared for the unknown difficulties that will come in life and ministry if he consistently grows in Christ day by day.

A spiritually rewarded life

Taken together, all these reasons to grow in Christ find their zenith in the event called the "bema" seat judgment (1 Corinthians 3:11-15). All believers in Christ will have an evaluation day with Jesus Himself. Our lives will be assessed as to the quality of what we "built." Since the foundation of this building is Christ, we can safely assume that to build with "gold, silver, precious stone" would be using more of the same material found in the foundation. Such a "building" can withstand Divine scrutiny while the edifices erected by lesser material (wood, hay, stubble—things of human origin) are consumed in the evaluation process. The reasons to grow in Christ enunciated above feed into this over-arching goal for every believer. We should want to stand before Christ and learn that we did indeed build our life and ministry on Him, for Him, and with Him. This can only happen when we purposely work at growing to think and act more like Christ day by day.

Peter also referenced the motivation of this day of reward with the words of II Peter 1:11, "For so an entrance will be supplied to you *abundantly* into the everlasting kingdom of our Lord and Savior Jesus Christ." Given all of God's truth regarding salvation, we understand that this is not teaching that our diligence *earns* us a spot in heaven. Rather our diligence earns us an "*abundant*" entrance to heaven. The works that survive judgment (1 Corinthians 3:14) can be abundant or scarce. Through diligent growth in Christ, we can have a large reward waiting for us in heaven.

Those who take their walk with Christ seriously may balk at such motivation as selfish, but it should be understood in the context of pleasing our Savior. If we desire to show our appreciation for our salvation by dedicated service rising out of a growing life in Christ, the result will be a larger reward. Can you imagine getting to heaven, standing in front of Christ for a life review (II Corinthians 5) and thinking, "I wish I'd done less to be like Christ, I wish I had served Him less in the Church, I wish I had taken more vacations and stayed home from church more often"? Peter is joyfully proclaiming that God has given us all things that pertain to life and godliness—even the way to earn His recognition on that Bema seat day. What could be more important and valuable than that?

Spiritual growth is achievable

When I was a boy, my father would occasionally check in at the end of a day and ask how many chapters of the Bible I had read. When I said "None," he would say, "That's too bad because I was going to give you $1 for every chapter you read." My father's heart was in the right place, but his plan was not helpful. I'm happy to report to you that your heavenly Father has not only revealed the imperative of spiritual growth for you but has made the path to achieving growth crystal clear. In the coming chapters we will work our way through that plan so you can have a fuller understanding of how to move forward in your life, your family, and your ministry.

Ideas/Questions For Application

1) On a scale of 1 - 10 (where 10 is best) how much effort do you give to your own spiritual growth?

2) List the specific activities you currently do as part of your effort at growth:

3) Does the value you place on spiritual growth mirror the value God places on it as enunciated in this chapter?

4) Do you need to repent of your lack of effort at growth and commit yourself to a fresh pursuit of it?

Chapter 4

THE FOUNDATION OF GROWTH

I have served several police departments as a volunteer chaplain, one of which was in a small town next to a metropolitan city. One day I was called to an industrial area where the two cities shared a border. There was a fatal car crash, and the attending officers had opened a river drawbridge to protect the scene by stopping traffic. As I made my way toward the location, I realized I was on the wrong side of the open bridge. In those days before GPS, one of the officers from the larger city offered to lead me around to the other side of the bridge where I was needed. I followed him until he stopped in an unknown place and came back to my car and said, "Sorry, I don't know how to get there." I was dumbfounded as he got in his police cruiser and drove away, leaving me to my own devices. Eventually I made it to the scene, but not without a fair amount of time-wasting wandering.

God has not left us to wander about seeking how to grow in Christ. He has made the path clear, but unfortunately, some of us were born again in a church or family that didn't have a robust understanding of the means of spiritual growth. From my observation in the counseling setting with many believers including some pastors and their wives, it appears that a good number of churches and academic Bible education ministries may fall into this category. I would assume that all believers understand some elements of spiritual growth, but many are missing a full grasp of the truth about developing a life in Christ.

As I mentioned earlier, I see a divine irony in God's use of the Apostle Peter to record a detailed path of spiritual growth. In the gospel narratives Peter is portrayed as a man with great zeal for the Lord but little strength of character, which leads to several significant failures that most Christians can readily recite. Decades later as he writes his final inspired words, we are learning from a man who became strong as he applied the truth he will share with us in his final message.

2 Peter 1:1-11

Simon Peter, a bondservant, and apostle of Jesus Christ, to those who have obtained like precious faith with us by the righteousness of our God and Savior Jesus Christ:

Grace and peace be multiplied to you in the knowledge of God and of Jesus our Lord, as His divine power has given to us all things that pertain to life and godliness, through the knowledge of Him who called us by glory and virtue, by which have been given to us exceedingly great and precious promises, that through these you may be partakers of the divine nature, having escaped the corruption that is in the world through lust.

But also, for this very reason, giving all diligence, add to your faith virtue, to virtue knowledge, to knowledge self-control, to self-control perseverance, to perseverance godliness, to godliness brotherly kindness, and to brotherly kindness love. For if these things are yours and abound, you will be neither barren nor unfruitful in the knowledge of our Lord Jesus Christ. For he who lacks these things is shortsighted, even to blindness, and has forgotten that he was cleansed from his old sins.

Therefore, brethren, be even more diligent to make your call and election sure, for if you do these things, you will never stumble; for so an entrance will be supplied to you abundantly into the everlasting kingdom of our Lord and Savior Jesus Christ.

Peter's audience

The Apostle Peter is writing to born-again believers in Jesus Christ as Savior. Several phrases make this abundantly clear, the first of which is in v. 1. Peter writes to those who "have obtained like precious faith." That is to say, the recipients shared his transforming faith in Christ. In v. 3 Peter states that both he and his readers have been given everything necessary to live a godly life. He is not calling them to *enter* the godly life, rather he will teach them how to *live out what they already possess*. In v. 4 he identifies his readers as those who have *already* been given the ability to partake in the divine nature and have *already* been given the ability to escape the ruinous impact of an unbelieving society. This passage is written for believers. It is not intended to explain how an unbeliever may come to faith in Christ even though it refers to that salvation in many ways.

Peter's burden for spiritual growth

The broad purpose of the book of 2 Peter is summarized in the second-to-the-last verse, "You therefore, beloved, since you know this beforehand, beware lest you also fall from your own steadfastness, being led away with the error of the wicked" (3:17). Peter begins this emphasis on protection from spiritual attacks in 2:1 when he warns of the danger of false prophets. In 3:3 he expands that warning to include spiritual scoffers. Peter is fully aware of the existence of such men who misinterpreted God's truth according to their own thoughts and desires. He personally experienced the hatred for the Christian faith which began during the earthly ministry of Christ and has continued unabated ever since. He was party to the challenges to pure doctrine which began shortly after the birth of the church, such as we see in Acts 15, that have likewise flourished in ever new forms throughout the intervening centuries.

Peter writes this book shortly before his anticipated death (1:14) to those he had discipled to give a final word of warning and a path of protection against the haters and heretics that were already on the scene and those yet to come. The intent of his message closely parallels that of Paul to the Ephesian elders in Acts 20:29 where he warns of "savage wolves" coming into the body of Christ to pervert believers from a genuine walk in Christ to a man-made religion. The urgency of this message heightens our anticipation of what Peter believes will provide the protection his disciples would need. The answer to our expectation is found in 2 Peter 3:18, "But grow in the grace and knowledge of our Lord and Savior Jesus Christ." Peter ends his final message as he begins it, urging spiritual growth. In 1:1-11 he said that believers ought to grow in Christ because of the great privilege they have to be like Him. He ends the book instructing Christians to grow so they won't be led astray to a pseudo-Christianity by false teachers.

Peter's exhortation to spiritual growth

With a heart of deep concern for the protection of his disciples, Peter urges his readers to capitalize on the gift of salvation God has given them. He wants to be certain they understand that the fullness of Christlike character ("divine nature" 1:4) in them will only come through their Spirit-empowered personal effort. He begins this challenge in vs. 4 with the words "you may become," which translates a single Greek word written here in the aorist subjunctive form, which indicates something that is, "possible, contingent upon certain conditions."[1] That contingency is the application of God's Word. When an individual is born-again, they are indwelt by Christ (Galatians 2:20) and are thus able to

---

[1] Summers, Ray. *Essentials of New Testament Greek.* Nashville, Tennessee: Broadman Press, 1950, 107.

manifest the righteousness of Christ but only through the application of God's Word. This is why Peter is so emphatic to use the word "diligent" twice (1:5, 10) in his exhortation, indicating that effort will be required in the process.

Peter shows deep concern for this truth about spiritual growth in 1:12-13 when he says, "For this reason I will not be negligent to *remind* you always of these things, though you know and are established in the present truth. Yes, I think it is right, as long as I am in this tent, to stir you up by *reminding* you." The readers of Peter's letter didn't have the privilege that we have of a complete leather-bound copy of God's Word (nor one on their digital device of choice!), thus such apostolic reminders were invaluable.

In Hebrews 2:3-4 we see a reference to God's New Testament revelation in these words, "How shall we escape if we neglect so great a salvation, which at the first began to be **spoken by the Lord**, and was **confirmed to us by those who heard Him**, God also bearing witness both with signs and wonders, with various miracles, and gifts of the Holy Spirit, according to His own will?" Luke enlarges our understanding of this aspect of revelation in Act 1:2-3, speaking of Christ, "Until the day in which He was taken up, after He through the Holy Spirit had **given commandments** to the apostles whom He had chosen, to whom He also presented Himself alive after His suffering by many infallible proofs, being seen by them during **forty days and speaking of the things pertaining to the kingdom of God**." This sentence nonchalantly tucked in between more noticeable truths tells us that Jesus spent 40 days teaching the apostles who in turn taught their disciples AND eventually wrote down the truths God wanted recorded. Although the common disciple had no book, they had much truth.

Peter refers to his previous verbal communication of God's Word which he believed was so important that he committed the truth to writing so they might be clearly known, remembered, and implemented. By God's plan, this message was Peter's final recorded inspired exhortation. God thought it was important for His children to grasp how spiritual growth happens in a clear concise communication. He could have moved Peter to restate the gospel message or to urge us again to love and good works, or He could have caused Peter to reveal some new depth of one of the cardinal doctrines of the faith, but He did not. Instead, He caused Peter to enunciate something that no other passage of Scripture says in quite the same way.

Peter's explanation of spiritual growth

Growth is initiated by effort

2 Peter 1:5-7 contains the action steps in Peter's message, that is, the *how* of spiritual growth. Right up front the instruction contains a command that on the surface might sound counter-intuitive, "Be diligent to *add* to your faith." Peter is not teaching us that we must do something to complete the removal of our sin; rather, he is expressing one of the cardinal doctrines of the Christian life, which is this; Christlike character is only developed through Spirit-empowered, Scripture-informed effort. Salvation comes to an individual in an instant of belief, by the gracious gift of God, but the character of the indwelling Christ only grows in the believer through Spirit-empowered effort over a lifetime.

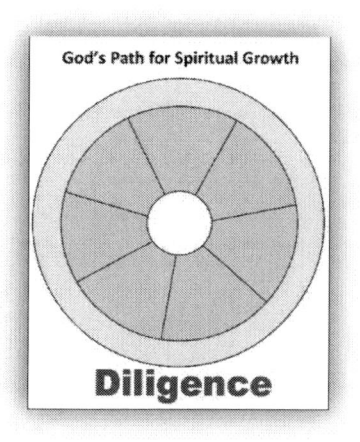

God freely gives salvation with no works or payment asked or accepted, but He created spiritual maturity to require the believer's effort. Peter uses the phrase, "like precious faith" to refer to salvation, and "the divine nature" to refer to the Christlike character implanted at salvation in all believers. The "faith" is something possessed at salvation, while our new life is something implanted at salvation which must be developed over a lifetime. The two-fold reality of the Christian life is summarized in Hebrews 10:14, "For by one offering He has *perfected forever* those who are *being* sanctified." When one believes in Christ they are completely and permanently saved from their sin. Yet there is an ongoing work of sanctification[2] or spiritual growth throughout their lifetime. It is not one or the other, but both.

Peter's command to be "diligent" has a root meaning of "hasten,"[3] and it comes first in the word order of the original language, making it very important. This is a word that might be used to indicate how one responds to a command. The picture that comes to my mind is that of a teenage boy being asked to take out the garbage. Does he do it with "haste" or sloth? Does he ignore the command and hope it will go away, or does he do as requested in the time expected? The Christian who is "diligent" hears God's instruction and goes to work applying it to his or her life without delay.

Gaining the life of Christ ought to be pursued like the gold in the hills of California was sought by men seeking their fortune a century and a half ago. While work is involved, Christlike character is the reward! The possibility of becoming like Christ makes this not so much work, equated only with toil, but effort to be expended in the pursuit of a great treasure.

Spiritual growth is made possible by the implanted life of Christ which comes as a result of salvation, but it only becomes a reality through diligent effort. As we continue our study of

---

[2]The root meaning of "sanctification" (translated from the word "holy") can be understood from the divine command recorded in 1 Peter 1:16, "Be holy, for I am holy." God commands the believer to be like Him. Thus, to be in the process of being sanctified means that one is becoming like God in character. The word in Hebrews 10:15 is a present participle indicating an ongoing action.
[3]Thayer, Joseph Henry. *Thayer's Greek English Lexicon of the New Testatment.* Grand Rapids, Michigan: Zondervan, 1974, 585.

Peter's plan for growth, we will learn how we are to exert diligent effort in partnership with our sanctifying Savior.

Chapter 5

THE ACTIONS OF GROWTH

Growth occurs through a process

The word "add" in 1 Peter 1:5 comes from a Greek word with a root meaning of "supply" or "furnish."[1] One of the recorded uses of it in ancient Greek literature was in reference to the theater, "to furnish the chorus at one's own expense; to procure and supply all things necessary to fit out the chorus."[2] The image is of a patron or producer who made sure all the costumes and props were supplied for the performance of a play and thus implies "supply" or "furnish" in a full way. The diligence God is commanding in this verse is directed at utilizing the virtues that follow in the text so that one's life in Christ (the result of faith) might be "fully furnished."

At first glance many would see this list of Christlike character traits as a shotgun blast of virtues to be acquired. Such lists are common throughout the New Testament. Colossians chapter 3 is an example with a list of sins to stop in v. 5, 8, and 9, and list of godly behaviors to start in v. 12-25. However, there are two key differences between the typical New Testament list of traits and this one. The first distinction is the **unique grammatical structure.** The first phrase in v. 5 begins with, "Be diligent to *supply* your faith *with* virtue." Then each subsequent word in the list is similarly phrased, "...and in the virtue, the knowledge, and in the knowledge, the self-control," etc. The word "supply" or "fully furnish" is assumed with each word

---

[1]Thayer, Joseph Henry. *Thayer's Greek English Lexicon of the New Testament.* Grand Rapids, Michigan: Zondervan , 1974, 246.
[2]Ibid., 246.

based on the first phrase, "Supply virtue to faith, and supply knowledge to virtue," etc. Rather than being a shopping list of Christlike behaviors, each word is connected to the previous as one might see water cascading over a series of terraces on a hillside. Everything flows out of faith and enables Christlike character as it flows fuller along the way. Commentator David Helm put it this way:

> The first three verses (v. 5-8) are commonly referred to as a list of virtues. In reality they are much more, for when things are merely placed in a list, each item stands independently, each has an identity of its own. Here, however, each characteristic is connected to what follows. In fact, the repetition of each word demonstrates that Peter intends for us to view them as inseparably linked to one another. In light of this, even the sequence in which they appear matters...to put an image on it, we could liken verses 5-8 to a golden chain or to stairs that lead one to the stars. Each stair or characteristic is built upon the strength of the previous one. And each subsequent one rises to a higher plane.[3]

Another commentator put it this way,

> Peter lists seven qualities of traits of character in this moral development, and he introduces each new trait as being "in" (*en)* "in connection with," the preceding. Each is inherent in its predecessor, which is in turn ***supplemented and perfected*** by the new quality, giving it more abundant fruitage.[4]

---

[3]Helm, David. *1 & 2 Peter and Jude.* Wheaton, IL: Crossway Books, 2008, 195.
[4]Hiebert, D. Edmond. *Second Peter and Jude.* Greenville, South Carolina: Unusual Publications, 1989, 52.

The virtues which God tells us to acquire are listed in a progression from the beginning point of faith to the culmination of love. This unique passage has been given to us by God to help us understand *how* we are to accomplish the task of sanctification. As we work through vv. 5-7, we will see that this is a path to growth which can be experienced as a linear process at times but could also be compared to a recipe which necessitates that all the ingredients be present for the desirable baked food to be produced.

The second distinction in this list is the **broad nature** of the virtues commanded. In Colossians 3 the sins to be put off are very specific, i.e., fornication, covetousness, anger, filthy language, etc., but in 2 Peter 1:5-7, the spiritual possessions to be pursued are varied in type and broad. "Knowledge" is not a single character issue but a comprehensive synonym for God's truth. One could only assume it is more of the knowledge referred to in 1:3 (which we will examine more fully as we work through the text) which asserts that it is the "knowledge of Christ" that comes through the Scripture which transforms the believer. This word implies a vast array of truth to be learned as opposed to one specific thought to put on. The term "self-control" is a more specific command but also has a wide impact as do the other terms. The understanding and application of these terms will be seen more fully as we work through them one by one.

Growth rises out of life

The fact that Peter put the word "diligent" first and "faith" second assumes that the recipients of his letter are already born-again. They have the enablement he enumerated in v. 1-4 because they have "obtained like precious faith" and are thus able to build on that faith (1:5). The word "faith" is used in several ways in Scripture, sometimes as an action we take and other times, as here, something we possess. Paul wrote to Timothy and referenced, "the genuine *faith that is in you*, which dwelt first in your grandmother Lois and your mother Eunice, and I am persuaded is in you also" (2 Timothy 1:5). Faith in Christ is the beginning of the Christian life, "No other foundation can be laid than...Christ Jesus" (I Corinthians 3:11). This "faith" which is the beginning point of Christlikeness is a synonym for salvation.

When we believe in Christ as Savior, He takes up residence in us, as Paul testified in Galatians 2:20, "I have been crucified with Christ; it is no longer I who live, but Christ lives in me," as does God the Father, "For you are the temple of the living God. As God has said: "I will dwell in them and walk among them" (2 Corinthians 6:16), and the Holy Spirit, "Or do you not know that your body is the temple of the Holy Spirit who is in you?" (1 Corinthians 6:19). Subsequent to salvation, as the believer gives effort to obey God's Word, he is cooperating with the Triune God at work within him to create the character of Christ.

As an intern between my fourth and fifth years of Bible college I met a young adult man whom I admired. He was tall, handsome, well-liked, and athletically talented. He helped with the summer ministry for which I was responsible. At the end of the summer, I went back to Bible college, and he moved on in his life. Later in the fall I received the church newsletter which listed those getting baptized, including him. I inquired about his plan to be baptized, and he replied, "Dave, I was just kidding myself," referring to the lack of the reality of salvation in his life. This man grew up in a loving, godly family, in a good Bible preaching church, made a profession of faith, and was baptized earlier in life, yet somehow managed to live with just a physical conformity to Christian behavior, or a mental assent to the truth, but he possessed no heartfelt transforming belief. He was not a deceiver or false teacher, but simply a man who had not come to a soul-deep faith in Christ. He is not the only person I have known to travel this road to discipleship.

The wonderful reality for those who have a genuine faith in Christ is this, "For you did not receive the spirit of bondage again to fear, but you received the *Spirit of adoption* by whom we cry out, Abba, Father. The Spirit Himself *bears witness* with our spirit that we are children of God" (Romans 8:15-16). Dear reader, is the Spirit of God bearing witness with your spirit that you are indeed a child of God? A different test of our faith is found in 1 John where he emphasizes the congruity of a claim to spiritual life with its evidence in righteous behavior, that is, if we claim to be Christians (literally "ones belonging to Christ"[5]) then we should be living like Christ. That test is equally important but can be hard to apply to oneself, especially for a man in vocational ministry. He may look at all he is doing as evidence of walking in Christ, when the reality is that he is just a religious man as those Christ spoke of who were not true disciples (Matthew 7:21-23).

I return to my question, is the Spirit of God bearing witness with your spirit that you are indeed a child of God? I know you can fake this, but why do so? You need to put your faith in Christ for your own benefit AND because your self-deception will not stop with you. It will affect your family and your flock. I am asking you to look in your soul and make sure it is one with the Father through the Savior, confirmed by the Spirit. If it isn't, put this book down, call a trusted friend, and work this out above all. Do not be concerned with keeping your reputation, your job, or anything else. "For what will it profit a man if he gains the whole world and loses his own soul" (Mark 8:36). Dear reader, are you in Christ?

---

[5] Brown, Colin, ed. *The New International Dictionary of New Testament Theology Volume 2*. Grand Rapids: Zondervan, 1976, 331.

I realize that the target of this work is those in full-time Christian ministry, yet I persist in asking the question. Are you in Christ? Is Christ in you? Do you have a settled faith in Christ as your Savior? If not, might this be the reason you have struggled to manifest a growing Christlike character? Might this be why your attempts to lead a congregation have been so difficult?

Growth requires obedience

"Add to your faith, virtue." The root meaning of the Greek word translated "virtue" is defined variously as, "moral excellence,"[6] "any excellence of a person...any particular moral excellence,"[7] "moral excellence,"[8] "God's attribute of perfection."[9] As with many New Testament Greek words a more thorough understanding of the root concept comes from its usage in various passages, especially with a word like this which is only used five times in the New Testament[10] with two of them in this passage.

In 2 Peter 1:3 we learn that believers have been given, "all things that pertain to life and godliness, through the knowledge of Him who called us by glory and *virtue*." This

---

[6] Vine, W. E. *Vine's Expository Dictionary of Biblical Words.* Nashville, TN: Thomas Nelson, 1985, 661.
[7] Thayer, Joseph Henry. *Thayer's Greek English Lexicon of the New Testament.* Grand Rapids, Michigan: Zondervan, 1974, 73.
[8] *The MacArthur New Testament Commentary, 2 Peter & Jude.* Chicago, IL: Moody, 2005, 40.
[9] Brown, Colin, ed. *The New International Dictionary of New Testament Theology Volume 3.* Grand Rapids: Zondervan, 1978, 927.
[10] Smith, J.B. *Greek-English Concordance to the New Testament.* Scottdale, PA: Mennonite Publishing House, 1955, 40.

reference to our Savior asserts that His effective call of salvation to us is based on "glory and virtue." Since the only persons ascribed intrinsic glory in the Bible are the three Divine persons, we understand that "glory" is a reference to the Divinity of Christ[11] while "virtue" refers to the sinless life of Christ. Peter gives a complete description of Christ in this brief statement when he references His glory and virtue.

Christ was able to call us to salvation *by His Divine power* (*glory*) over sin, death, hell, and the grave which was made possible by the sacrifice of *His perfectly righteous life (virtue)*. The question remains of what such moral excellence means when addressed to the believer in a command. The simplest understanding would be that Christians are expected to live a life of *virtue*, that is, to live as Christ did—righteously. Since we are not able to add intrinsic moral excellence to the salvation given us by Christ, and since this word is in a list of qualities to be diligently added in one's walk with Christ, I would assert that it is a used as synonym for "obedience." M.R. Vincent sees a similar thought,

> Not in the sense of moral excellence, but of the *energy* which Christians are to exhibit, as God exerts his energy upon them. As God calls us by his own virtue (v. 3), so Christians are to exhibit *virtue* or *energy* in the exercise of their faith, translating it into vigorous action. (*emphasis* in original)[12]

After being born-again, the believer is to seek to live like Christ. Simply put, he or she is to do whatever thought or deed they know to be righteous. Given all the other words in this progressive list of virtues, I would paraphrase the beginning of v.

---

[11]"In Scripture glory always belongs to God alone…Thus when sinners see the glory of Christ they are witnessing His deity." *The MacArthur New Testament Commentary, 2 Peter & Jude.* Chicago, IL: Moody, 2005, 29.
[12]Vincent, M. R. *Word Studies in the New Testament Volume 1.* McLean, Virginia: MacDonald Publishing, 1886, 324.

5 like this, "Because God has given believers the ability to possess the character of Christ, they should give diligent effort to obey all that they know to be righteous like Christ."

Growth is defined by knowledge

The next step in this progressive path of spiritual growth is to learn more of God's definition of righteousness. The word translated *knowledge* is used throughout the NT to refer to that which may be known, "especially spiritual truth,"[13] "...the divine truth that is the foundation of spiritual discernment and wisdom,"[14] "the general knowledge of the Christian religion."[15] We learn of this word from the Apostle Paul's desire in Philippians 3:8, "I also count all things loss for the excellence of the *knowledge* of Christ Jesus my Lord." Peter circles back to this same word and idea at the end of his epistle when he says, "Grow in grace, and in the *knowledge* of our Lord and Savior Jesus Christ" (2 Peter 3:18). The knowledge that Christians must have to grow is the knowledge of Christ, both His person and His instruction.[16]

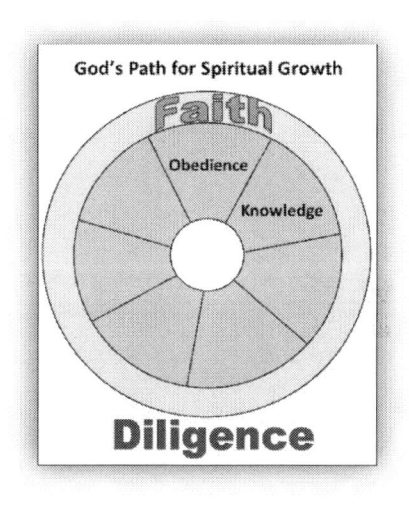

---

[13] Vine, W. E. *Vine's Expository Dictionary of Biblical Words.* Nashville, TN: Thomas Nelson, 1985, 348.
[14] *The MacArthur New Testament Commentary, 2 Peter & Jude.* Chicago, IL: Moody, 2005, 40.
[15] Thayer, Joseph Henry. *Thayer's Greek English Lexicon of the New Testatment.* Grand Rapids, Michigan: Zondervan, 1974, 119.
[16] "To whom He (Jesus) also presented Himself alive after His suffering by many infallible proofs, being seen by them during *forty days* and speaking

At first glance, it would hardly seem necessary to exhort a pastor to "add knowledge" in his walk with Christ. Knowledge is the stock in trade of the preacher. Most men go to school for a minimum of four years and many for more. Such schools focus on useful educational activities like listening to lectures, reading books, writing papers, and taking tests to help the prospective pastor gain knowledge of the Scriptures, but the knowledge Peter is exhorting us to is more than academic Biblical/theological content. A summary of 2 Peter 1:3-5 with emphasis added will help us define the "knowledge" spoken of in v. 5; "His divine power has given to us **all things that pertain to life and godliness**, through the **knowledge of Him** who called us by glory and virtue, by which have been given to us **exceedingly great and precious promises**, that through these you may be **partakers of the divine nature**, having **escaped the corruption** that is in the world through lust" (2 Peter 1:3-4).

The growing believer must pursue the knowledge God has given in His Word that enables him to be transformed from the ruinous ways of unsaved society into a Christlike disciple (v. 4). Greek and Hebrew word definitions enable an accurate understanding of God's Word. History sets the stage for understanding language and culture. Systematic theology helps a Christian to discern the truth, but the goal must be to know that which enables him to become more like Christ.

The path to that kind of knowledge requires approaching the Word of God as pictured in several metaphors God uses to teach us about His truth. One of those pictures is of a mirror and teaches us that God's Word helps us mature in Christ by its ability to show us what we really look like. "If anyone is a hearer of the word and not a doer, he is like a man observing his natural face in a mirror; for he observes himself,

---

of the things pertaining to the kingdom of God" (Act 1:3). Jesus taught the Apostles *after* His resurrection, and they subsequently shared this truth as well as what we read in the gospels.

goes away, and immediately forgets what kind of man he was. But he who looks into the perfect law of liberty and continues in it and is not a forgetful hearer but a doer of the work, this one will be blessed in what he does" (James 1:23-25). God's Word is the mirror we look at to see the dirt that needs to be removed from our face, the hair that needs to be combed, the shirt that needs to be rebuttoned, and the pants that need to be changed because they don't match the sweater.

John Piper, in his popular book on the Christian life, quotes extensively from George Müller who was a man greatly used of God in the 19th century. In his lifetime he created orphanages that cared for over 10,000 children and 117 schools of Christian education which trained over 120,000 students. He was instrumental in distributing over 285,000 copies of the Bible, 1.5 million New Testaments, and over 244,000 other religious books. His ministry raised and distributed over 113 million dollars to worldwide missions. And this is what he had to say about seeking God's transforming truth (**emphasis** added, italics were in the original):

> "The point is this: I saw more clearly than ever that the first great and primary business to which I ought to attend every day was to have **my soul happy in the Lord.** The first thing to be concerned about was not, how much I might serve the Lord, how I might glorify the Lord; but how I might get my soul into a happy state, and how my inner man might be **nourished.** For I might seek to set the truth before the unconverted, I might seek to benefit believers, I might seek to relieve the distressed, I might in other ways seek to behave myself as it becomes a child of God in this world; and yet, not being happy in the Lord, and not being **nourished** and **strengthened** in my inner man day by day, all this might not be attended to in a right spirit.

Before this time my practice had been, at least for ten years previously, as an habitual thing, to give myself to prayer, after having dressed in the morning. *Now* I saw that the **most important thing I had to do was to give myself to the reading of the Word of God** and to meditation on it, that thus **my heart might be** comforted, encouraged, warned, reproved, instructed, and that thus, whilst meditating, my heart might be **brought into experimental** *(*we would say "experiential*)*, **communion** with the Lord. I began therefore, to **meditate** on the New Testament, from the beginning, early in the morning.

The first thing I did, after having asked in a few words the Lord's blessing upon His precious Word, was to begin to meditate on the Word of God; searching, as it were, into every verse, to get blessing out of it; **not for the sake of the public ministry** of the Word; **not for the sake or preaching** on what I had meditated upon; but for **the sake of obtaining food for my own soul**. The result I have found to be almost invariably this, that after a very few minutes **my soul has been led to confession, or to thanksgiving, or to intercession, or to supplication;** so that though I did not, as it were, give myself to *prayer*, but to *meditation*, yet it turned almost immediately more or less into prayer.

As the outward man is not fit for work for any length of time, except we take food, and as this is one of the first things we do in the morning, so it should be with the inner man. We should take food for that, as everyone must allow. Now what is the food for the inner man: not *prayer*, but the *Word of God:* and here again **not the simple**

> reading of the Word of God, so that it only passes through our minds, just as water runs through a pipe, but considering what we read, pondering over it, and applying it to our hearts...[17]

Truth to feed the soul is what every believer needs regularly. I am fully aware that God did not command us to read the Word daily, so I will not try to manipulate God's truth to say so. I am equally aware that we are not told that we must be in the Word first thing in the morning. However, I would offer some thoughts from the Scripture for consideration. The Psalmist wrote, "O God, You are my God; Early will I seek You; My soul **thirsts** for You; My flesh **longs** for You in a **dry** and **thirsty** land where there is no water." (Psalm 63:1) and "As the deer pants for the water brooks, So pants my soul for You, O God" (Psalm 42:1). Every time we feel anxious, overtaxed, fearful, or burdened is a time of "panting for the water brooks" of God. We need what only God can give to refresh our souls, so why would we not be in the Word daily and early, that is before all other activity as Müller did?

One of the problems for pastors seems to be the belief that there is so much needed daily ministry activity that he must give his greatest attention to it immediately. This subtle shift in thinking causes a man to believe he is serving God all day according to God's desires. Such a pattern may be the result of forgetting the words of the King of Israel, called, "a man after God's own heart," (Acts 13:22) when he wrote Psalm 51:16-17, "For You do not desire sacrifice, or else I would give it; You do not delight in burnt offering. The sacrifices of God are a broken spirit, A broken and a contrite heart, these, O God, You will not despise." This must have been radical when it was first prayed or sung out loud. Was David saying the Old Testament worship system of sacrifice was unimportant? NO. He was saying that

---

[17]Piper, John. *Desiring God.* New York: Multnomah, 2011, 154-156.

having one's heart right with God must come before and with external spiritual activity.

Even more common is the sentiment voiced by Müller that the pastor goes to the Word to get material for a sermon or some other public ministry rather than going to it as food for his own soul. I am quite aware of the ideology which asserts that a man's time in the Word as he studies to preach is his time with the Word so that he doesn't need a separate time. To the extent that happens, it is a good thing. However, I know that once a man is in his study at his desk preparing to preach, a hundred things can grab his attention and he can be consumed in study or some other aspect of church work, but not truly be focusing on his own soul as he should. Having an appointment with God first thing in the morning in a place without interruptions ensures that a man will be able to look God in the face and commune with Him through the Word and prayer[18] and be prepared for what will come his way that day.

I was recently in a church service focused on the ordination of a man for the gospel ministry. His pastor (a man of several effective ministries over decades) gave the "charge to the candidate" which was based on the challenge to, "keep your heart" (Proverbs 4:23). One of the applications of this verse was an exhortation to have his daily personal time in the Word in a **different book** of the Bible than he was currently preaching. He explained that this would help him consider his own life and hear what God might to say to him personally. I could not agree more.

Müller's sentiment of getting his soul into a "happy state," and of seeking food or nourishment for his soul, is vitally important for the man of God. Surely, I am not the only pastor who feels that ministry drains his spiritual battery as he gives to his people. Am I the only pastor who has been tired on a Monday after teaching Sunday School, leading worship,

---

[18]The practice of prayer in this process of growth will be addressed later.

preaching, interacting with the flock, and doing one or more ministries on Sunday evening? If such fatigue is normal (and I believe it is), how does one feed the spiritual hunger and strengthen the pastoral muscles? Through time with the Lord in His Word.

Jesus promises to meet the needs of life *if* we attend to His priorities, "Seek first the kingdom of God and His righteousness, and all these things shall be added to you" (Matthew 6:33). The question is, do we believe the words of Jesus enough to start the day by communing with Him? Do we see the need to meet with Him? Another Christian of the 19th century, one of the greatest missionaries of all time, Hudson Taylor, who very much depended on God, said it this way, "Do not have your concert first, and then tune your instrument afterwards. Begin the day with the Word of God and prayer and get first of all into harmony with Him."[19]

In our first mentoring meeting, I asked a pastor about his practice of spending time with the Lord, and he relayed this anecdote. He had to get up very early to travel to another city to hear a renowned speaker and so he did not spend time in the Word and prayer that morning. One of the first things he heard from the speaker was a question to the listeners about their daily time with the Lord. He observed that if they skipped their time with Christ to be on time to hear him that they made a horrible exchange.

My new bride and I enjoy our time together. There are times when either her activities or mine keep us apart for a while, but we always enjoy coming together again when the opportunity returns. Would you really rather get right to work without spending some quiet moments with Christ? Do you love to study so much that you don't want to look Christ in the face and hear from Him personally before you start the day?

---

[19]Chandler, Otis, ed. *Good Reads*. n.d. tps://www.goodreads.com/author/quotes/4693730.James_Hudson_Taylor.

Oh brother, your time with Him IS THE foundation of your life and ministry. Make a plan right now for spending time in the Word daily. If you need an idea of how to do so, you can see appendix #1 at the end of this book where I have outlined my plan or you can speak to some of your brothers and ask how they spend time with the Savior, but above all, get started.

Growth is enacted by planning

The word "self-control" has a root meaning of exactly what it sounds like, "to have control over oneself."[20] It only occurs six times in the NT and presents somewhat of a conundrum. One of the other notable uses of this word is in the list of attributes which the Holy Spirit produces in the believer; "The fruit of the Spirit is love, joy, peace, longsuffering, kindness, goodness, faithfulness, gentleness, *self-control"* (Galatians 5:22-23). As a serious but immature believer at age 19, finally trying to grow in Christ, I wondered whether it was the Holy Spirit's work to give me self-control or my responsibility to control myself. The answer is provided by another passage of Scripture which does not use this term but does enable us to understand God's intent for our practice. The sixth chapter of Romans explains the believer's relationship to sin and righteousness. I summarize some of the truths here:

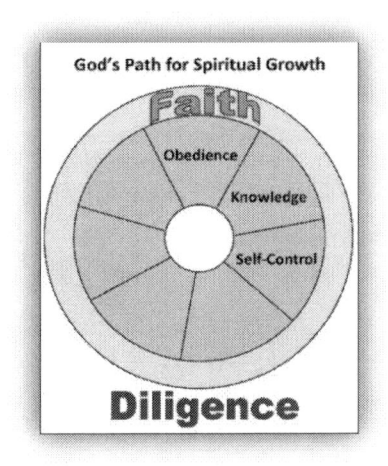

- The believer is dead to sin (Romans 6:2) and has been freed from its power (6:7).

---

[20]*The New International Dictionary of New Testament Theology Volume 1.* Edited by Colin Brown. Grand Rapids, MI: Zondervan, 1975, 494.

- The believer is organically connected to Christ in his death, burial, and resurrection resulting in the breaking of sin's power and the infusion of the life of Christ (6:3-6).

- The believer must "reckon" (KJV/NKJV), "count" (NIV) "consider" (NASB), that is, agree with or genuinely believe these truths (6:11).

- The Christian who truly believes them will apply them by not "*presenting*" aspects of his life to sin but instead "*presenting*" all aspects of his or her life to God to do righteousness (6:13).

- The way a believer exerts spiritual self-control is to take account of his thoughts and behaviors and create plans to *stop* those which are sinful and *replace* them with righteous ones, and then to *act on those plans* based on the reality that Christlike character is achievable.

In Peter's path to Christlike character, knowledge itself is not the goal, rather, knowledge enables the believer to move toward the goal of Christlike character as it is applied or practiced. For this to happen, *self-control* is required. "In 2 Peter 1:6 it (self-control) follows 'knowledge' suggesting that what is learned requires to be put into practice."[21] "The list exhibits the movement by which faith comes alive and becomes fruitful in love, *enkrateia* (self-control) is here hardly to be understood in an ascetic sense (to simply bear down and force oneself to do something). The term is used rather in its original meaning of having power over oneself, not however on the basis of some supposed self-realization, but on the basis of the knowledge which comes from faith (vs. 5-6)."[22] Spiritual self-control, rather than an oxymoron, simply means to purposefully act on the

---

[21]Vine, W. E. *Vine's Expository Dictionary of Biblical Words.* Nashville, TN: Thomas Nelson, 1985, 620.

[22]Brown, Colin. *The New International Dictionary of New Testament Theology.* Edited by Colin Brown. Vol. 1. Grand Rapids, MI: Zondervan, 1975, 497.

truth that we are free to do righteousness by careful evaluation *of* and planning *for* needed change.

A plan to apply the Scriptural instruction must begin with confession. "If we confess our sins, He is faithful and just to forgive us our sins and to cleanse us from all unrighteousness" (1 John 1:9). The pastor who would live in Christ must not let sin linger. As soon as a believer sins, they are walking under the influence of their sinful human mind and heart. When a believer allows sin to remain, more sinful choices are made and life spirals down into greater ungodliness. This is exactly what God asserts in Galatians 6:8, "He who sows to his flesh will of the flesh reap corruption, but he who sows to the Spirit will of the Spirit reap everlasting life."

This is my personal plan (I call it a ***rule*** for me): **confess the first sin immediately.** Although I try not to, I sin every day, and I do my best to confess *every* time. I do not let sin remain. I want the joy and peace of Christ, not the shallow substitutes which I might be tempted to accept. The pastor who allows sin to remain risks creating problems in his church through a personally sinful life, a humanistic (perhaps academic or legalistic) preaching of God's truth, and faulty leadership decisions made in the flesh. I could tell stories (not my own, thank the Lord) of fists put through walls, children punched in the face, and grudges carried for years all because of the lack of a close walk with Christ. I interviewed a pastor who became angry at God when his church voted against his desired change in the ministry. Instead of confessing his anger, he held it closely, quit spending personal time with God in the Word and prayer, increasingly gave into actions he had avoided, and conducted pastoral activity out of his human talents for several months until he committed adultery because he had no strength to say "no" to a pursuing woman.

A heart right with God is ready to hear God's instruction *(knowledge)* fresh each morning and apply that instruction to create change. For instance, when a man reads, "I say to you that whoever looks at a woman to lust for her has already committed adultery with her in his heart" (Matthew 5:28), he must admit his temptation and create some method to turn from it. Such a rule might be as simple as turning your eyes in the opposite direction of the object of temptation. Personal rules like this work best when accompanied by prayer for help from God. We fail to be righteous when our go-to is rational consideration without prayer. It is not hard for a man to convince himself that a sin is not really that bad or maybe not wrong at all. In regard to sexual lust, I have heard men say, "Just because you are on a diet doesn't mean you can't look at the dessert." Such men must have missed this verse, "If your right eye causes you to sin, pluck it out and cast it from you; for it is more profitable for you that one of your members perish, than for your whole body to be cast into hell" (Matthew 5:29).

Thought life is only transformed by substituting the truth of God for sinful thinking. When a believer is plagued with anxiety, he needs to seek those truths in the Word that answer his worried mind and heart. Passages like Matthew 6:19-34 offer a series of principles that calm the struggling heart. Those who struggle with anxiety would do well to read the Matthew passage frequently, praying the thoughts out to God (as in Philippians 4:6) and would greatly benefit from memorizing such a passage and repeating it in prayer to God when the storms of life seem to rage about.

These are only *examples* of how a believer can **plan** to think and act righteously. As you consider your work of shepherding in the coming chapters, greatest benefit you will receive will come by making plans to work on areas of needed growth. Part of your plan for growth must include the next four virtues in the path, as they will be critically important to spiritual transformation.

Growth is realized by perseverance

All three of my children played youth soccer but one of them gave up quickly with this observation, "I don't like to run that much." Unlike many other competitive sports, soccer has a clock that stops rarely, which means that the players must be ready to be in motion for the duration. When I see the word "perseverance" in this list of virtues on the path of growth, I have the same question as I do with the term "self-control." Is perseverance a sort of soccer field "tough it out and suffer through it" kind of self-discipline or is there a spiritual dimension? Since God never tells us to do anything in our human strength, there must be more to genuine spiritual perseverance.

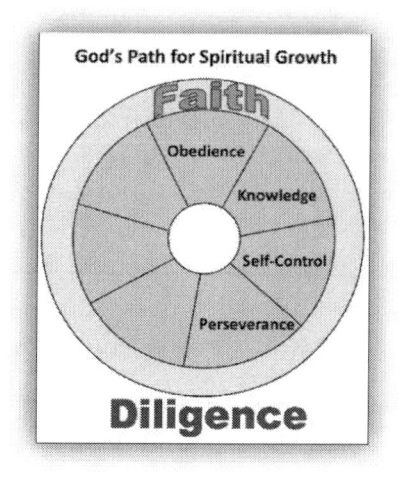

The word "perseverance" (NKJV, NIV, NAS), is also translated "patience" (KJV). This Greek word is sometimes translated "endurance" (NASB) or "steadfastness" (ESV). It is a compound word composed of two words, "stay" and "under." Other translations include "to remain,"[23] "patient, persevere, endure."[24] A paraphrase of the passage may help us more clearly understand the intent of this word at this point; A believer (*faith*) learns a new way to act like Christ (*knowledge*), so he creates a plan to act on that knowledge (*self-control*) and then must practice it, over and over and over (*perseverance*).

---

[23]Thayer, Joseph Henry. *Thayer's Greek English Lexicon of the New Testatment.* Grand Rapids, Michigan: Zondervan, 1974, 644.
[24]Brown, Colin, ed. *The New International Dictionary of New Testament Theology Volume 2.* Grand Rapids: Zondervan, 1976, 764.

As the believer works to "stay under" this piece of knowledge, transformation is accomplished by the Holy Spirit. A new behavior becomes a character trait not just by repetition but by the power of God transforming him through that obedient repetition as we read in 2 Corinthians 3:18, "But we all, with unveiled face, beholding as in a mirror the glory of the Lord, are being *transformed* into the same image from *glory to glory,* just as by the Spirit of the Lord." Following the path of growth causes the believer to progress from one level of Christlikeness to another as he or she obeys the promptings of the Spirit through the Word of God. Practicing this truth requires that we run to the Father in prayer for strength and wisdom (James 1:5).

One of my pastor-brothers lost his wife of 50 years quite suddenly. At the memorial service he described the debilitating impact of grief that would come on him unexpectedly AND he relayed how that all he could do was call out for help to God. When he did this he said the impact was palpable, "I felt it [relief] in my body." Instead of retreating into self-pity and allowing sadness to overtake his life, he called on God and effectively *persevered* through the trial. Having gone through the loss of a spouse myself, I understand that there will be more than a one-time need to pray for help. This repeated doing of what is right and calling on God for help is the stuff of spiritual perseverance. As we do this we are transformed (II Corinthians 3:18). This is the very thing that the Apostle Paul had to do:

> 1 Corinthians 9:24-27 Do you not know that those who run in a race all run, but one receives the prize? Run in such a way that you may obtain it. And everyone who competes for the prize is **temperate** *(self-controlled)* in all things. Now they do it to obtain a perishable crown, but we for an imperishable crown. Therefore, I run thus: not with uncertainty. Thus, I fight: not as one who beats the air. But **I discipline** *(perseverance)* my

body and bring it into subjection, lest, when I have preached to others, I myself should become disqualified.

There are many truths that can encourage us in our perseverance. Chief among them would be Hebrews 12:1-2,

> "Therefore we also, since we are surrounded by so great a cloud of witnesses, let us lay aside every weight, and the sin which so easily ensnares us, and let us run with **endurance** *(perseverance)* the race that is set before us, looking unto Jesus, the author and finisher of our faith, who for the joy that was set before Him **endured** the cross, despising the shame, and has sat down at the right hand of the throne of God."

The fruitful pastor focuses on the joy of pleasing His Savior by transformative obedience, in every personal and pastoral challenge, which enables him to shepherd the local flock of Christ effectively.

One of my sons-in-law came to help me remodel a bathroom. We tore it down to the studs then started installing the new bathtub. We plumbed in the drain then placed the tub, but the pipes did not match the tub. We took it out and made adjustments, more than once, and finally gave up for the evening right after he said, "I've never done this before." Now you tell me! There is no need for a pastor to be frustrated regarding how to honor the Lord with his life and ministry, because God has given us clear guidance as to what he expects and how to move toward it.

God wants men who would lead His people to be growing in Christlike character which begins with genuine faith in Christ as Savior. It proceeds with obedience to known instructions, then seeks to learn more of God's expectation, and implement those truths through careful planning and endurance. Along with this clear path, God offers His strength to empower our obedience. We will consider that power in the next chapter.

Chapter 6

THE POWER OF GROWTH

While the Apostle Peter does not specifically mention prayer in his formula for growth, we know he believed in the importance of it from exhortations he wrote in his first epistle. However, the foundational truth expressed in 2 Peter 1:4, "Whereby are given unto us exceeding great and precious promises: that by these ye might be partakers of the divine nature," clearly implies ALL of the empowering promises of God including answering the prayers of believers for spiritual growth.

The New Testament promise of God's help through prayer begins with the instruction of Jesus to the apostles regarding how to pray, "In this manner, therefore, pray: our Father in heaven, hallowed be Your name. Your kingdom come. **Your will be done** on earth as it is in heaven. Give us this day our daily bread. And **forgive us** our debts, as we forgive our debtors. And **do not lead us into temptation** but deliver us from the evil one. For Yours is the kingdom and the power and the glory forever. Amen" (Matthew 6:9-13). The highlighted phrases illustrate the importance that requests like these from the model prayer can have on our walk with the Lord.

One of the greatest reasons to pray is found in Romans 8:26, which says, "Likewise the Spirit also **helps** in our weaknesses." The word "helps" means to, "take hold with another."[25] The image is of two people lifting a heavy load

---

[25]Thayer, Joseph Henry. *Thayer's Greek English Lexicon of the New Testatment.* Grand Rapids, Michigan: Zondervan , 1974, 601.

together. In particular in this passage, the weakness is our human perspective in prayer which causes us not to make requests to God as Jesus would, that is "in His name" (John 16:26). However, our weaknesses go far beyond not knowing the right way to pray. We need all kinds of strength, wisdom, and guidance that only our Divine Helper can give, and that assistance must be sought in prayer.

    As Peter unfolds his formula for growth (1:5-7) he begins with the possession of salvation (faith) without which no spiritual growth is possible. Then he moves to obedience (virtue) as the primary and recurring steps which every believer must take. Then he moves to knowledge (learning more steps of growth), self-control (plans to act on the knowledge gained), and perseverance (determined repetition that leads to the Spirit's transformation).

    Throughout the implementation of these steps in the formula, prayer is needed, but I have waited till this point to include an exhortation to it because there is a danger in connecting prayer with spiritual progress. That danger is the practice of some who pray for growth but do not exert effort as exhorted in this passage and others. These well-intentioned Christians have either ignorantly or erroneously believed that victory over sin is wholly a work of God. In a very insightful article, commentator Andrée Seu Peterson exhorts the reader to be certain that repentance goes beyond feeling bad about sin. She laments the common teaching in some Evangelical circles which seems to ignore the personal responsibility of the believer to actively participate in sanctification. "The aversion comes from a theological commitment to the idea that God must do everything, and we must do nothing. It sounds theologically lofty, protective of God's sovereignty, and like a bulwark against works righteousness or the notion of earning grace. But as a matter of fact, the Lord does give us many things to do. *Doing* is not the same as *earning* [emphasis in the original].[26]

It is also likely that some people pray for growth and do not understand their responsibility to work at it, or how that should be enacted. Perhaps Peter focuses on the believer's responsibility to actively pursue growth, without including prayer (and uses the word 'diligent' twice!), to make it extra clear that active effort is required. I have chosen to place my emphasis on prayer at this point in our study for a similar reason. We note that faith is the beginning of the path of spiritual growth, followed by obedience, knowledge, self-control, and perseverance, which must all be saturated in prayer to be divinely effective.

My emphasis on prayer will not come with an exposition of all the riches of the Scripture regarding prayer as this has been thoroughly done by men of much greater eloquence than me. However, no discussion of spiritual growth would be complete without an admonition to prayer. Every aspect of the believer's life and ministry should be brought before the Lord. A brief review of the New Testament Epistles instructs us about the importance of prayer:

- Prayer is part of the process of growth (Jude 1:20).

- Prayer brings God's help to withstand temptation (Matthew 26:41).

- Prayer is a vehicle for worship (Hebrews 13:15, Philippians 4:6).

- Prayer is part of the antidote for anxiety (Philippians 4:6-7).

- Prayer is a source of strength for humility in ministry (1 Peter 5:5-7).

---

[26]Peterson, Andrée Seu. "A Step Beyond Surrender." *World Magazine*, March 23, 2024: 70.

- Prayer is part of a right response to spiritual adversaries (Ephesians 6:10-18).

- Prayer is a primary response to illness (James 5:14-16).

- Prayer is a source of strength for ministry (Ephesians 6:19, 2 Thessalonians 3:1, Colossians 4:3).

- Prayer is a source of deliverance from difficulty (Philemon 1:22, Philippians 1:9).

- Prayer is a primary response to civil authorities (1 Timothy 2:1).

- Prayer is a primary response to needs and desires in ministry (1 Thessalonians 3:10).

- Prayer empowers our efforts to help believers become mature in Christ (Colossians 4:12, Ephesians 1:16).

God has commanded us to pray (1 Timothy 2:8, Matthew 6:9, 1 Thessalonians 5:17) and told us the many ways that He will empower life and ministry in response to our prayers. No amount of spiritual activity can accomplish what only prayer can make happen, AND no amount of prayer can take the place of our God-commanded effort at growth. They are two sides of one coin. The believer who will not make time for prayer will live an impoverished spiritual life as will the believer who prays but exerts no effort to grow and serve.

No one has a greater need to pray than a man who is leading a group of believers. The fruitful pastor must be a man of prayer just as he must be a man of the Word. He will pray for himself, his family, his church, his community, and the greater world. In my experience, this will only be accomplished by some method of journaling. Very few of us have photographic memories and so we need to have lists of those life circumstances, people, and ministry needs for which we ought to pray *SO we can be exhaustive* in expressing our concerns to God, thereby living in His peace (Philippians 4:6-7).

At the end of every first counseling session, I ask the counselees to tell me about their plan for spending time in the Word and in prayer on a daily basis. Most have no plans for spending time with the Lord, and of those who do have a plan many do not have a prayer list, including those pastors I see in this setting. When I ask if they are praying for the specific challenges and problem people from their life we are discussing in counseling, they often say "no". No wonder they are not making progress in their life. God has promised His help *through* prayer. We should not be surprised that the lack of prayer results in an anemic or degenerating life. The critical beginning point to a vital prayer life is a written list on which we work to be exhaustive with our concerns (Philippians 4:6 "everything"). Such a list is also very helpful as we are able to write notes of completion when God answers our prayer. How else can we be faithful at appreciating the work of God like the solitary leper who came back to Jesus after his prayer was answered.

A Pastor who wants to call in the forces of heaven to his life and ministry must have a method of remembering his prayer concerns, a daily time of focused prayer, and a growing discipline of handing each concern to God in prayer as the day progresses. I offer my journaling method as part of **Appendix "A"** only as an example and hopefully to stimulate your thoughts of how you can organize your prayer life. I stress that there may well be other excellent ways to be a faithful pray-er. The only wrong way is to fail to pray.

Following God's path to growth requires purposely implementing the steps outlined by Peter with prayer. As we go forward we will complete Peter's formula that refers to several relationships that are vital in carrying out the actions of obedience, knowledge, self-control, and perseverance.

Chapter 7

THE RELATIONSHIPS OF GROWTH

Relationship with God

The next term in Peter's path of spiritual growth turns our attention to motivation. The word translated "godliness" is used only a few times in the New Testament. It is variously translated as "worship,"[1] or "To reverence, to shrink back in fear."[2] Vincent notes that "This quality is never ascribed to God."[3] This is a word compounded from two words, "well' and "devout." At first glance, the English translation, to be "godly", seems to be instructing the believer to act like God. However, this occurrence stands in contrast to other terms like, "*godly sincerity*" (2 Corinthians 1:12), which implies acting like or being like God in one's sincerity.

Rather than *acting like God*, the root idea in "godliness" is *devotion **to** God* which **motivates** one to act *like* God. Vine

---

[1]Robertson, A.T. *Word Pictures in the New Testament.* Vol. 6. Nashville: Broadman Press, 1933, 149.
[2]Brown, Colin, ed. *The New International Dictionary of New Testament Theology Volume 2.* Grand Rapids: Zondervan, 1976, 91.
[3]Vincent, M. R, *Word Studies in the New Testament Volume 3.* McLean Virginia: Mac Donald Publishing CO, 1886, 324.

agrees with this when he writes, "It denotes that piety which, characterized by a Godward attitude, does that which is well-pleasing to Him."[4] MacArthur sees the same thing when he asserts that this word means, "reverence for God...and conveys the idea that one who has it properly honors and adores God."[5] This root idea of godliness means that the growth process is not just becoming like Christ in character but growing in our respect or reverence of God. To respect God means that the believer does not choose his own path but that which has been given to him by God, out of a heart *devoted to* God. It means that the Christian's love for God is measured by the command of Jesus to, "Love the Lord your God with *all* your heart, with *all* your soul, with *all* your mind, and with *all* your strength" (Mark 12:30).

    This kind of devotion to God is vital in the process of growth. As the believer learns more of God's truth (*knowledge*) and plans how to implement that truth (*self-control*) there will be many tests and temptations that cause him to question whether he should *persevere* on that path. At such moments the believer must draw strength by remembering his commitment to God based in what Christ did for him, as Paul said:

> For I am the least of the apostles, who am not worthy to be called an apostle, because I persecuted the church of God. But by the grace of God, I am what I am, and His grace toward me was not in vain; but I labored more abundantly than they all, yet not I, but the grace of God which was with me. (1 Corinthians 15:9-10)

    Paul was motivated to carry on with God through difficult time, rejection, and ministry which seemed ineffective

---

[4]Vine, W. E. *Vine's Expository Dictionary of Biblical Words.* Nashville, TN: Thomas Nelson, 1985, 272.
[5]MacArthur, John. *The MacArthur New Testament Commentary, 2 Peter & Jude.* Chicago, IL: Moody, 2005, 42.

because he owed God his very soul. Hiebert summarizes the connection between these truths well when he says, "Christian endurance is motivated by "*godliness,*" that attitude of reverence that seeks to please God in all things...Godliness brings the sanctifying presence of God into all the experiences of life."[6]

Relationship with Fellow Believers

As Peter continues his teaching on how to grow in Christ, we come to a character trait which we often see more as a goal than a means to the goal of Christlikeness. This is another compound Greek word composed of the word "brother" and a word for "affection." Most Bible translations chose a consistent way to translate this word to keep it separate from the more well-known word for love, "agape." The NKJV, KJV, NIV, and NASB translate this term as "brotherly kindness" while two of the newer translations chose "brotherly affection" (CSB, ESV). This word is best understood in contrast to the more common word for love, agape. The prime characteristic of agape love is sacrifice while this word focuses more on relationship, hence the "brother" half of the word. This kind of love arises from the shared human condition. As fellow human beings we understand what it is like to be sick, happy, hungry, impoverished, or to experience many other common challenges by which we are able to sympathetically relate to our fellow human beings.

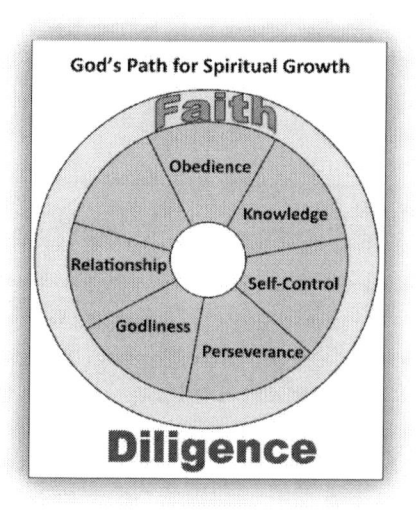

---

[6]Hiebert, D. Edmond. *Second Peter and Jude.* Greenville, South Carolina: Unusual Publications, 1989, 54.

As we consider the intent of this term in this list, we must remember that God has given us a progressive path for growing in Christlike character. When we factor out the implications of the other terms, we realize that there is something inherent in "brotherly love" that supports spiritual growth. Instructions like this come to mind, "Bear one another's burdens, and so fulfill the law of Christ. For if anyone thinks himself to be something, when he is nothing, he deceives himself" (Galatians 6:2-3). This implies that there are times when the believer is not able to fully bear his burden by himself. Without the help of other Christians, he may well fail to grow as God desires.

God's intention for believers, known collectively as the "Body of Christ," is that our interaction should reflect our singular reality spoken of in 1 Corinthians 12:12; "For as the body is *one* and has many members, but all the members of that *one body*, being many, are *one body*, so also is Christ (v. 21) And the eye cannot say to the hand, 'I have no need of you;' nor again the head to the feet, 'I have no need of you' (v. 25) that there should be no schism in the body, but that the members should have the *same care* for one another." God intends the Christian life to be lived out in *community* with other believers as one commentator noted, "The godly must cling together like so many brothers of one family, like so many friends, in close friendship and friendliness."[7]

How does this command help the believer grow in Christ? Relationships among believers provide instruction, encouragement, accountability, and affirmation as we take steps on our path toward Christlike character. This is a two-way street affording us the help we need and the opportunity to help others as they grow, but only if we invest in relationships with our brothers and sisters. Hebrews 10:24-25 summarizes this truth beautifully, "And let us consider one another in order to stir up love and good works, not forsaking the assembling of ourselves

---

[7]Lenski, R. C. H. *The Interpretation of St. Peter, St. John, and St. Jude.* Minneapolis, MN: Augsburg, 1966, 269.

together, as is the manner of some, but exhorting one another, and so much the more as you see the Day approaching."

There is great irony in a man whose job and calling are to help others grow spiritually being unwilling to ask for help with his own walk with Christ! Men in general and pastors in particular seem reticent to ask for help with spiritual issues because of the real or perceived weakness it communicates. I counseled a pastor who nearly succeeded at suicide. I was one of the first calls he made for help AFTER he was revived and hospitalized. From previous interactions, he knew me well. Why didn't he ask for help during the months of struggle which led up to the attempt to end his life? I know of a pastor who had an accountability partner in his church and flat-out lied to him on the path to having an affair. Even after being confronted with needed change, many men will not open themselves to a brother who could help them progress. This is nothing more than pride and fear. What would a pastor say to a parishioner who needed yet refused such help?

One of the most important helpers in a pastor's spiritual growth should be his wife. Godly spouses (in any home, not just that of a pastor) ought to be helping each other know the truth and carry it out. The one who lives with a man knows when things are off and may even inquire about circumstance. But will the help be received which God sends through our sister believer?

Beyond one's spouse, the fruitful pastor can benefit greatly from the input of a brother pastor who can help with life's challenges without being overwhelmed to find out that the preacher has feet of clay. No one understands ministry life like a brother who is a pastor. I have been part of a network of likeminded churches in my region since I entered full-time ministry. Forty-six years of relationship-building has provided men with whom I can share the joys and sorrows of ministry. Our network has three annual gatherings which provide a venue for ongoing interaction and support when needed. There were men before me in my position to whom I reached out to for guidance, and now it is my privilege to be available to encourage others. I was once asked to help in a time when a man was asked to resign. This man told me, "I wanted to reach out for help, but I felt sheepish to do so as I had never connected with the network." If he had called and received the wisdom offered, he might have avoided the errors that led to his resignation.

There are certainly other ways to build supportive relationships. You could find a professional mentor, coach, or counselor. You could reconnect with a friend from college/seminary days with whom you can build a relationship that goes beyond surface friendship (I have found this to be very helpful in some critical decisions). You could approach a mature man in your circle of churches and ask him to mentor/counsel/coach you (we will talk more about this later).

I realize that a growing pastor will not need the help of a brother all the time, but there will be times when the burden is too large to bear alone. God says that we should let others help us in those moments. We do not need to suffer or struggle in isolation! 1 Corinthians 12 makes it clear that individual believers are not meant to live life alone. You need a fellowship of men in your life. Ask God to help you find or create it.

Relationship with self

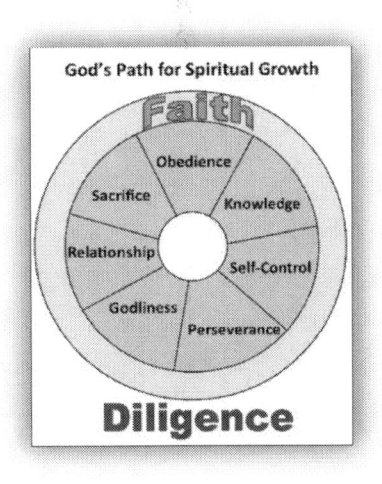

The final command in this dynamic instruction is that the believer is to add "love." *Agape,* which is perhaps the most familiar New Testament Greek word to contemporary Christians, was almost unknown in the noun form in the common Greek vocabulary of the first century. The verb form, "*agapao*," was more widely known and meant, "to honor or welcome."[8] Again, we must turn to Scripture to help us more clearly understand God's use of this word. The most concise definition is given in 1 John 3:16, "By this we know love, because He laid down His life for us. And we also ought to lay down our lives for the brethren." The key concept in this kind of love is doing what is needed for the one loved even if it means the sacrifice of self.

Spiritual growth demands sacrifice. Every act of obedience requires the believer to lay down his own fleshly life so he can put on the thoughts and behaviors of Christ. The sacrifice may be setting aside personal preferences to care for another believer. God may ask us to let go of closely-held family ties to move to a distant place of service. Many (dare I say all) pastors will be called upon to give of their time and let go of financial desires to follow God's call. Most pastors will encounter unjust criticism which may never be requited in this life.

The sacrifice of oneself is necessary in the process of growth. The believer must say no to self and yes to God. He must be willing to accept all that God allows in life without regard to self-driven desires, and he must put others first. If Paul was right when he wrote, "The greatest of these [gifts of God to the believer] is love" (I Corinthians 13:13), then the epitome of spiritual maturity is love. In this list, this is not a quality to obtain after we acquire all the other traits of godliness, rather it is a consistent action in as we grow moment by moment gradually manifesting more of the divine nature.

Sacrificial actions are empowered by focusing on the end results of our choices in this life and the next. Again, our Savior is our prime example in this as in all things:

> Therefore we also, since we are surrounded by so great a cloud of witnesses, let us lay aside every

---

[8]Brown, Colin, ed. *The New International Dictionary of New Testament Theology Volume 2*. Grand Rapids: Zondervan, 1976, 538.

weight, and the sin which so easily ensnares us, and let us run with endurance the race that is set before us, looking unto Jesus, the author and finisher of our faith, who **for the joy** that was set before Him **endured** the cross, despising the shame, and has sat down at the right hand of the throne of God. (Hebrews 12:1-2)

The "joy" set before Christ was the salvation of us poor sinners. Christ endured the multi-faceted hardships of His limited earthly life; oppression, death, and burial *because* of the incredible good that would come from it. All adults do this every day when they set their short-term desires aside and get up and go to work so they can get a paycheck, some non-cash benefits, and a retirement plan. Surely those of us called to lead God's work can stay focused on the results of souls saved and lives transformed *now* AND God's reward for our service *later* so that we might consistently grow to be more like Christ!

The Application of Growth

Growth is accomplished by effort

As Peter concludes his teaching on how to grow in Christ, he once again emphasizes the effort that is required, "Therefore, brethren, be *even more diligent...*" (2 Peter 1:10). Peter wanted his readers to fully grasp the importance of their own effort in following God's path for growth.

With a foundational understanding of this process, we will now turn our attention to using it to accomplish spiritual growth. This is the "proactive" use of this process that guides the believer to greater Christlike character.

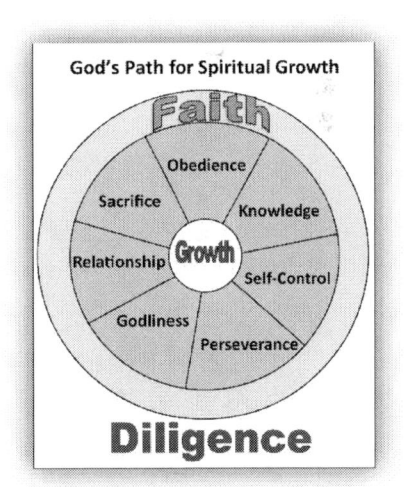

As such it is a *linear application* of the truth. That is, progress in any area of life happens as we apply these principles, one after the other, to that issue or character trait which needs to develop.

There is also a "reactive" use of this process as well which I referred to earlier as a "recipe." In my counseling ministry (which I would summarize as highly personalized discipleship) I have seen that in any lack of spiritual maturity, or any problem thought or behavior, one or more of these ingredients of growth are either unknown or unused by the struggling believer. Through careful interaction those deficits may be realized and corrected as the Christian is willing. In the chapters that follow, I will endeavor to help you see how this process can help you grow in Christlike character and ministry.

I have had joint replacement in both knees (and a hip and a shoulder). The process went like this: I was taken into the operating room, fell asleep with anesthesia, and woke up with a new knee, a lot of swelling, and a fair amount of pain. Once I was fully awake the nurse got me up and helped me walk. On day two I went to physical therapy where I was instructed to use a rubber band to bend my knee by pulling my heel toward my back side while seated in a special recliner. It hurt and the therapist verbally (and physically) pushed me to bend it as far as possible which increased my pain substantially. Every day that I was in the hospital I repeated this painful exercise, and I was also urged/commanded/cajoled into walking laps around the hospital floor. I was instructed to keep up the therapy exercises at home, and one week later I began treatment with a physical therapist who pushed me harder and farther until I regained near-full mobility and strength.

It is a great privilege to live in an era in which arthritic joints can be replaced, but surgery is just the starting point. A strong pain-free life requires diligent exercise which is well worth the time, pain, and cost. Salvation in Christ gives us a wonderful new life that holds the prospect for a joyful, peaceful journey, but this potential, given by God in our new life, is only realized by much diligent effort. Peter knew that personally, and his exhortation was that the time, pain, and cost would be eternally worthwhile.

With this process of growth in mind, how do we know what we should be working on? The Christ life encompasses all of our waking time and serving as a pastor includes many kinds of activity. How can a man who wants to be a fruitful pastor know what to emphasize in his desire to grow?

Besides making thoughtful evaluations and plans for progress, every pastor will be led to grow by God through His universal method of stimulating spiritual growth, which we will consider in our next chapter.

Questions/Ideas for Application

1) Write your own summary of the process of growth from 2 Peter 1:5-7. Spend some time thinking it through and work toward memorizing this "recipe" for growth.

2) Go back to these evaluations from chapter 1 and reconsider them in light of the path to growth:

3) If you are an aspiring pastor, evaluate how ready you are for a pastoral role. Prayerfully consider (in conjunction with input received from others) what further preparation, mentoring, or experience might help you be more fully prepared. Keep these areas of needed growth in mind as you consider personal and pastoral growth in the rest of this book.

4) If you are a seasoned pastor, evaluate your life and ministry and choose some targets for growth. If you do not see any blatant weakness, you might spend some time in a passage of scripture like 1 Timothy 3 seeking the direction of the Holy Spirit regarding needed growth. Keep these in mind as you read the next few chapters which are focused in detail on how to grow in Christ.

5) Take an honest look at your where you are at in life and note two or three areas in which you need to progress. Analyze the growth areas according to Peter's plan. Which elements are missing? Make a plan for progressing in each area.

Chapter 8

THE DIRECTION OF GROWTH

Joy was the shortened version of Joyce that a church member had taken as her preferred moniker, which was exceedingly ironic given her normally negative outlook. She was divorced and well into retirement years with a single adult child who suffered through the few interactions with her mom that she could not avoid. Once I called on Joy in the hospital when she had a serious surgery. After visiting, I offered to pray before leaving, which she gladly accepted. As was often my practice, my prayer did not focus on healing but instead reflected the thoughts of Moses in Psalm 90: 16, "Let Your work appear to Your servants, and Your glory to their children." My prayer included words to the effect that God would make Himself known in her circumstance. When I finished, she said, "That's an odd prayer." I explained that many people in similar circumstances would be whining and complaining and miss the opportunity to represent God to the staff and other patients. Joy responded, "I'm like that," which I had hoped she would recognize thus giving me the opportunity I needed to encourage her to honor God in this trial.

One of the themes I see consistently from struggling Christians is the lack of understanding regarding difficulty as a tool of God, and I find that pastors are not immune from this deficiency. When problems come, the average Christian believes that the most important outcome is the removal of the problem, whether it be a physical hardship, relational rough spot, or organizational breakdown, yet God's primary concern in such challenges is the spiritual growth of His children. The resolution (end) of challenges can and should bring God glory through the praise of His saints, but even more so should the growth that God intends to take place along the path to resolution.

Beyond this aspect of testing for all believers, there is a value in trials for a pastor which may not be readily recognized; that is, ministry skill or ability development through difficulty. When God allows or causes hardship, it should be viewed as His direction for growth, what one could call His "class assignments" whether they concern character or pastoral skill. One of the ways God reveals His agenda for our growth is through the challenges He brings across our path. For example, I am not naturally a compassionate person, I tend to see the need for personal responsibility rather than sympathy for those in difficulty. To help me grow, God led me into emergency service chaplaincy work even though I didn't fully understand what I was volunteering for. Once I got there, I was presented with the need to sympathize with people in unexpected critical hardships. I could have chosen to exit the work, but instead, I let it school me.

John 15:2 bears out this aspect of trials quite clearly. The Christian who is bearing fruit will come into hardship, which Jesus called "pruning;" that is, the shaping of the believer's growth for future service. Recognizing God's use of trials is vital, especially for pastors who are tempted to see ministry challenges as undeserved interruptions in the work they want to do for God. If not handled properly, the pastor's trials can lead to frustration, sin, ministry breakdown, and even death. I have witnessed numerous examples of men who have failed to deal with challenges, both personal and pastoral, in godly ways and are no longer in pastoral ministry. I have even seen spiritual immaturity and worldly thinking about trials leading to attempted suicide.

God moved Peter to communicate the divine *path of growth* for Christlike character development and He caused

James to let us know how God uses trials to *direct the use* of that path from day to day. Through difficulty and hardship God gives believers a divine impetus to spiritual growth.

> My brethren, count it all joy when you **fall into various trials**, knowing that the **testing of your faith** produces **patience**. But let patience have **its perfect** work, that you may **be perfect and complete**, lacking nothing. If any of you lacks **wisdom**, let him ask of God, who gives to all liberally and without reproach, and it will be given to him. But let him ask in faith, with no doubting, for he who doubts is like a wave of the sea driven and tossed by the wind. For let not that man suppose that he will receive anything from the Lord; he is a double-minded man, unstable in all his way. (James 1:2-8)

The definition: what is a trial?

The Greek word translated "trials" (**NKJV, NIV, NASB**) or "temptations" (KJV) is translated by both words in other verses in various translations. "The noun *peira*, 'attempt,' 'trial,' or 'experiment' (Pindar) and the vb. *peirao*, 'to test, try' (Homer, Il. 8,8) together with the intensive form (rare in cl. Gk.) *peirazo*, to tempt someone, put to the test (Homer, Od. 9, 281), come from the root *per.*"[1] The practical understanding of the word is not found in the definition alone. A more helpful discussion is here, "This poetic and late prose form of *peirao* (*peirazo*), even when used in the general sense of 'try', 'test', has always the idea of **probation** associated with it" [emphasis added].[2] Tasker picks up on this truth when he comments, "The Greek word...has the *double sense* of outward trials, and inward temptations. Outward

---

[1] Brown, Colin, ed. *The New International Dictionary of New Testament Theology Volume 3*. Edited by Colin Brown. Vol. 3. Grand Rapids, MI: Zondervan, 1978, 798.
[2] Milligan, J.H. Moulton AND G. *Vocabulary of the Greek Testament*. Peabody, PA: Hendrickson, 1997, 501.

trials very often **become** occasions of temptation to sin" [emphasis added.][3]

A fuller understanding comes by observing the word's usage in various Scripture texts which flesh out the intended theological meaning. In James 1 the "trials" of v. 2 are part of a larger thought connected with the word "testing" (*dokimon*) in v. 3 thus translated as a trial or test. In v. 13 "trial" is translated "tempted" because it is connected with internal sinful desires in v. 14. We understand the word "testing" (*dokimon*) more clearly from texts like 2 Corinthians 13:3 and Philippians 2:22 in which it is translated "proof" or "proven". Thus "trial" (James 1:2) is the **process** and "testing," v. 1:3 better translated "proving" or "being approved," is the intended **result**. Moo's comment is helpful when he says, "In the present verse, the use of *face* (NIV) (lit. 'fall into') and the replacement of *peirasmos* by 'testing' in verse 3 strongly favor the second meaning" [that 'trials' in v. 2 means external affliction].[4]

The determination: how do trials come to the believer?

Vital to understanding what trials are and how God uses them in the life of the believer is the recognition of when and how they happen. Our prime text, James 1:2, summarizes the reality of tests as something the believer *"falls into."* This word is defined as "to fall into as to be encompassed by."[5] The narrative in Luke 10:30 exemplifies the meaning, "Then Jesus answered and said: 'A certain man went down from Jerusalem to Jericho and *fell among* thieves...'" [emphasis added]. This traveling man was minding his own business and in modern terms was mugged. This mirrors the account of Job who was a devoted

---

[3]Tasker, R. V. G. *Tyndale NT Commentaries: The General Epistle of James.* Grand Rapids: Eerdmans, 1975, 40.
[4]Moo, Douglas. *Tyndale New Testment Commentaries.* Vol. James. Downers Grove, IL: Intervarsity, 2015, 80.
[5]Thayer, Joseph Henry. *Thayer's Greek English Lexicon of the New Testatment.* Grand Rapids, Michigan: Zondervan, 1974, 504.

believer who suddenly found himself "encompassed" (Thayer's definition of "fall into") by huge difficulties *not of his own making*.

This same dynamic is seen in an episode from Abraham's life, recorded in Hebrews 11:17, "By faith Abraham, when he was *tested*, offered up Isaac." Abraham "fell into" a faith testing challenge. Philip had the same experience recorded in John 6:5-6, "Then Jesus lifted up His eyes, and seeing a great multitude coming toward Him, He said to Philip, 'Where shall we buy bread, that these may eat?' But this He said *to test him*, for He Himself knew what He would do" [emphasis added]. Philip *fell into* a challenging circumstance.

It is important to note that not all trials have their original source in God, but they are still allowed and used by Him in the life of the believer. There are several notable Scriptural examples of the enemy of our soul, Satan, being the source of difficulty for the believer. The apostle Paul gave this testimony in 2 Corinthians 12:7, "And lest I should be exalted above measure by the abundance of the revelations, a thorn in the flesh was given to me, a *messenger of Satan* to buffet me, lest I be exalted above measure." We get another glimpse into the workings of God in the words of Christ in Luke 22:31 when He said, "Simon, Simon, behold, Satan hath desired to have you, that he may sift you as wheat." Clearly, Satan wanted to bring a trial to Peter and although we are not told if it was him, Peter was sorely tested not long after this interaction. Job is, of course, the prime example that pulls back the curtain on God's method of allowing Satan to cause the believer trouble. These examples make it clear that God is in control, but His purposes for the believer are sometimes advanced through the activities of Satan carried out with His full knowledge.

It should go without saying, but the very fact that God says trials are to be embraced as part of maturing in Christ means that they are not random occurrences. It has become fashionable in recent years for Christians to blame certain catastrophes and hardships on the sin that entered the world at the fall and has progressively ruined creation and societies ever since. The intent seems to be an effort to let God off the hook for such events, but it is not based in good theology. *God* tested Abraham. *God* allowed Job to be tested by Satan. *Jesus* tested Philip. *Jesus* also made it clear that those who are spiritually productive will encounter something He called "pruning" (John 15:20 thus Christ Himself causes challenges in the life of the dedicated believer as does God the Father.

The dynamic: how does God use trials?

While the word "patience" in v. 3, is translated variously as patience (NKJV), perseverance (NIV), and endurance (NASB), the root meaning of the compound word is "remain or stay."[6] If the outcome of trials is endurance and this requires the active participation of "staying" to accomplish, then the dynamic God employs in trials is **pressure**. "Stay" clearly implies that difficult circumstances create a desire to escape from under the trial yet that is what is specifically prohibited. "The only way out of a trial is through it. The Lord promises no bypasses, only that He always will see His people through the trials without their suffering spiritual harm."[7] We also note in 1:3 that the process of testing will produce patience, yet in the next phrase the believer is instructed to allow patience to have its perfecting work. Thus, God's process requires the believer's participation to accomplish its divine goal.

God tells us where to look for examples of how the faith-life works in Romans 15:4, "For whatever things were written before were written for our learning, that we through the *patience* (staying under) and comfort of the Scriptures might have hope." James uses this very principle in giving an example

---

[6]Brown, Colin, ed. *The New International Dictionary of New Testament Theology Volume 2*. Grand Rapids: Zondervan, 1976, 772.
[7]MacArthur, John. *James*. Chicago: Moody, 1998, 32.

of what "staying" looks like in vv. 5:10-11, "My brethren, take the prophets, who spoke in the name of the Lord, as an example of suffering and patience. Indeed, we count them blessed who **endure.** You have heard of the perseverance of Job and seen the end intended by the Lord—that the Lord is very compassionate and merciful." In the prophets and in Job, we see men of God act righteously while the trial was *pressing* on them. This wonderful testimony is given at one point of Job, "In all this Job did not sin with his lips" (Job 2:10). Joseph is another outstanding example of righteous living under various significant trials (Genesis 30-50).

Other Scriptural examples tell different stories. King Saul directly disobeyed the instruction of the Lord because of the desire to placate the unruly Israelites (1 Kings 15, especially v. 21). Samson caved in to his personal/sensual desires for a wife being unwilling to do it in the right way (Judges 14:1-3). John Mark couldn't take the heat of ministry and gave up midstream (Acts 15:38). What we see in these examples is that under the pressure of difficult circumstances, the growing believer will do what is righteous no matter how weighty the pressure. If we connect this back to the object of testing, the believer's faith, then we realize that God presses the believer to see how firmly he is committed to Him and His way of life. The obedient child of God continues in righteousness allowing God to shape him more into the image of Christ. "The RSV captures the active nature of this patience, calling it 'steadfastness,' for this is not a passive virtue but a ***steady clinging to the truth*** within any situation"[8] [emphasis added.]

The believer who follows God's plan, by staying under the trials, grows in spiritual endurance. It is vital to note that this obedience is transformative (2 Corinthians 3:18). The believer does not repeatedly grit his teeth and hang on till the trial is past.

---

[8]Kamell, Craig L. Blomberg and Mariam J. *Exegetical Commentary on the New Testament.* Vol. James. Grand Rapids: Zondervan, 2008, 49.

Rather, as the believer follows God's instruction he becomes more "perfect," that is, more like Christ.

The design: what does God want to accomplish through trials?

James 1:4 identifies the purpose of trials with the phrase, "that you may be **perfect** and **complete lacking nothing.**" "Perfect" means the "end, termination...that by which a thing is finished...the end to which all things relate, the aim, purpose."[9] "This expression can denote not only perfection but maturity."[10] Vincent agrees, "(Perfect) denotes that which has reached its maturity or fulfilled the end contemplated."[11] James couples "*perfect*" with "*complete*" which is a compound word from "'whole' and 'part', to give the idea of 'perfected all over' or 'fully developed in every part'."[12] The words "lacking nothing" (*complete*) seem superfluous in this three-fold statement of *perfect, complete,* and *lacking nothing.* Any of the words could have stood alone, but together they leave no room for debate in conveying God's absolute goal of full maturity in Christ for every believer.

The use of these words in other Scripture removes any obscurity about what God intends in their use by James. Perhaps the most challenging verse is Matthew 5:48, "Therefore you shall be *perfect,* just as your Father in heaven is *perfect.*" If that isn't clear enough, the Apostle Paul couches his instruction to the church to be lived out, "...until we all come to the unity of the faith and of the knowledge of the Son of God, to a **perfect man, to the measure of the stature of the fullness of Christ**"

---

[9]Thayer, Joseph Henry. *Thayer's Greek English Lexicon of the New Testatment.* Grand Rapids, Michigan: Zondervan , 1974, 618.
[10]Kamell, Craig L. Blomberg and Mariam J. *Exegetical Commentary on the New Testment.* Vol. James. Grand Rapids: Zondervan, 2008, 50.
[11]Vincent, M. R. *Word Studies in the New Testament Volume 2.* McLean Virginia: Mac Donald Publishing CO, 1886, 344.
[12]John F. Walvoord & Roy Zuck, Editors. *The Bible Knowledge Commentary.* Wheaton, IL: Victor Books, 1983, 821.

(Ephesians 4:13). God's goal in His use of trials in the life of the believer is to help him become like His Son, Jesus Christ. Not *similar*, but *exactly like* the righteousness of Christ. While specific trials will have specific purposes, the over-arching goal of trials for the Christian is to move him further down the road toward total Christlike character.

This goal will be fully realized only when believers see Christ face to face (1 John 3:1-2), but while we are yet in our human existence, the process of becoming like Christ is ongoing (Hebrews 10:14) and accomplished in part through the process of trials. Moo misses the point when he says, "Believers are asked to respond to trials with joy, then, because they know that they are working **to produce a deeper, stronger, more certain faith**" [emphasis added] (Moo 2015). Yes, trials are to deepen the faith of the believer, but the goal of that fuller faith is more Christlike character. Our goal is also the goal of Christ recorded in Ephesians 5:25-27, "Husbands, love your wives, just as Christ also loved the church and gave Himself for her, that He might sanctify and cleanse her with the washing of water by the word, that He *might present her to Himself a glorious church, not having spot or wrinkle or any such thing, but that she should be holy and without blemish.*"

It is vital to note that God's purpose (Christlike character for the believer) guides His causation or allowance of specific trials. Believers often struggle with the question of "why" something has happened to them. The answer is found in an often-misunderstood passage. Hebrews 12 is seen by many to reference the work of God in punishing His erring children. The word "chasten" (NKJV, KJV) creates the image of spanking a disobedient child. The NIV and NASB come closer when they use the word "discipline", but this also lends itself to the punishment motif. The root meaning of chasten, Greek "paideia," is "to train children."[13] While there are both negative

---

[13]Thayer, Joseph Henry. *Thayer's Greek English Lexicon of the New Testament*. Grand Rapids, Michigan: Zondervan, 1974, 473.

and positive implications in this word according to its usage, it is a great misconception to say that God *punishes* believers for their disobedience. Perhaps this comes from the common expression of human parents punishing their children for their defiance.

However, both are wrong. God punished Jesus for our sin (Isaiah 53:5) because we could not bear His wrath AT ALL. Instead of punishing believers for their missteps, God uses difficulty to prod the believer back onto the straight and narrow way AND He uses difficulty to direct our growth even when we haven't sinned. This is quite clear in Hebrews 12:10-11, "For they indeed for a few days chastened us as seemed best to them, but He for our profit, that **we may be partakers of His holiness.** Now no chastening seems to be joyful for the present, but painful; nevertheless, afterward it **yields the peaceable fruit of righteousness** to those who have been trained by it." God causes hardship, but He doesn't give punishment, rather the hardship is something intended to move us toward greater spiritual maturity. As such it parallels pruning. (And...good parents don't make their children pay for their disobedience. Rather, they give negative consequences of various kinds to cause children to make better choices in the future...just as God does for us.)

While I don't imagine that trees and plants feel pain, I could anthropomorphize them and ask the question, "Does it hurt when some part of the growing thing is cut off?" I have a relative who used to be an orchardist. He seems to know *everything* about growing apples! I learned that when the blossoms come on the tree, there are four blossoms together with a "*king" blossom* in the middle. The wise orchardist removes the center larger "king blossom," which allows the other four to produce bigger apples. If this pruning causes pain, might we also imagine that the larger fruit crop produces joy? I suspect that if I stood up in church and asked a congregation if they would like to be more like Jesus, that most of them would say, "Absolutely yes!" If I followed that question with, "Do you want to be like Jesus if it takes significant trials;" that they might be less enthusiastic. Trials are hard, but an increasing Christlike character is worth the pain.

The details: how does the believer experience growth in trials

Three imperatives[14] instruct the believer on how to benefit from trials. The first is in v. 2, "*count* it all joy." The believer is told to choose how he thinks about trials with a word that means "to lead."[15] Sometimes this word is used to literally mean, "lead," as in Matthew 2:6 or Luke 22:26. Other times it means to choose a perspective on reality as in Philippians 2:3 and 2:6. Human beings don't naturally think joyful thoughts about adverse circumstances. Such an ***attitude*** only becomes a reality in the believer by an active choice based on the whole truth of this passage and other Scriptures. The potential for this transformation of thinking is inherent in our salvation because it is part of, "the new man who is renewed in *knowledge* according to the image of Him who created him" (Colossians 3:10). God causes the mind of the believer to be reborn just as our heart and soul and someday our body will be. Believers have been freed from the sensual thinking of earth-bound humanity. It is possible to value Christlike character more than a comfortable life. As Christians align their values with their heavenly Father, they can obtain the joy of Christ (John 15:11) even in hard times.

The second command is in the word "patience" which we have previously understood to mean "stay" or more literally "stay under." The ***action*** commanded is in v. 4, "*let* (this is the

---

[14]An imperative is a Greek grammar "mood of command or entreaty—the mood of volition. It is the genius of the imperative to express the appeal of the will to will." We commonly refer to these as "commands." Mantey, Dana &. *A manual Grammar of the Greek New Testament.* Toronto: MacMillan, 1955, 174.

[15]Thayer, Joseph Henry. *Thayer's Greek English Lexicon of the New Testatment.* Grand Rapids, Michigan: Zondervan , 1974, 276.

imperative) patience have its perfect work." Staying under a trial "communicates the idea of cooperation with God's work."[16] Cooperation means embracing the value of the trial and not attempting to escape it. It should be obvious that there can be no sinful behavior chosen when one is attempting to cooperate with God. The answer to the hard marriage is not a new spouse. The critical church member cannot receive hate from the pastor he attacks. The financial shortfall must not be filled up by thievery. The godly believer lives consistently in righteousness—including during a trial.

  The third command is a directive of resource. Verse 5 assumes that the experience of trials will consistently bring the believer into circumstances in which they feel out of their depth. This sense of being overwhelmed is part of God's plan to drive us to Himself for **assistance**. God does not throw believers into the deep end of the pool just to see if they can swim. He does so to cause them to realize that they need the Divine lifeguard more than ever. The wonderful truth is that God stands ready to help if believers will ask. God instructs His children to ask for wisdom to help them stay in and work through the trial. Proverbs 3:5-6 comes to mind in this context, "Trust in the LORD with all your heart, and lean not on your own understanding; in all your ways acknowledge Him, and He shall direct your paths."

  The believer who desires to grow through trials *prays* to God to understand which Scripture should guide his behavior. Then armed with the knowledge of how to behave, he *calls on God* for help to do what is right. He may need to *ask God* how to bring multiple Scriptural principles to bear as there may be more than one Biblical instruction on how to relate to a person or circumstance. Above all, the growing believer *asks God* to empower His Word and to infuse His child with the very thing

---

[16] Swindoll, Charles. *James, 1 & 2 Peter*. Grand Rapids: Zondervan, 2010, 30.

most needed, endurance. As this process unfolds, new Christlike character is formed in the Christian.

The Process applied: What does this look like in pastoral life?

As a brand new 22-year-old, just out of college, green-behind-the-ears, enthusiastic associate pastor, I lived in an apartment in the church with my wife. On one of my first Sunday afternoons, I washed the car in the church parking lot in front of our apartment. Turns out, some folk thought that was wrong. Not long after this, the Senior Pastor relayed to me how someone deemed me unspiritual for sitting on the platform with my legs spread apart, rather than crossed as a gentleman would. Wow, really? Is this the stuff that bothers people? What's a young pastor to do? It didn't take many days in full-time ministry for me to experience trials that happened *because* I was in ministry.

Our church apartment came with a kitchen on the other side of the building, about 50 yards away. Soon a newly constructed kitchen was completed, right next to our apartment. Very accessible; however, we could not leave dirty dishes on the counter, especially on Sunday morning. The church refrigerator was our refrigerator, etc., etc., you get the idea. On the first facility workday, my job (assigned by the Senior Pastor) was to follow a very old man as he painted and clean up after him. I could go on with many small challenges, not to complain or generate sympathy, but to simply illustrate the truth that ministry brings *unique* trials.

There were also what I would call "medium" sized trials. For me that included how much I was paid, or the need to submit to my Senior Pastor who did not always do things as I did.[17] More than once he ridiculed me for taking a whole day off. His work patterns were different than mine. I often saw him

---

[17]Both he and his son have been in heaven for some time, so they won't mind me sharing!

in the office (I could see the lights from the street) on Saturday evening. While we conflicted at times, some of his impositions became lifelong ministry habits, like getting the name and address (and email and cell-phone number in later years) of every person who attends church. He pushed me hard on this until I saw the value.

We had no budget for youth ministry because we had a layman who vociferously opposed paying for "parties for the youth group." We were not allowed to do fundraisers as this was considered unspiritual ("God's people should give for the ministry") so I had to find creative ways to fund our youth work. I was accused by a parent of being "worldly" to attract young people to our programs. We had church member parents whose teens were very challenging to have in class or at an event.

Then there were some larger trials like having children on a meager salary and caring for them while conducting a very active youth ministry. Or the challenge of carrying on a full church program while helping build a new auditorium and classrooms. We had Sunday School in our house for a while with 30+ teens in our tiny living room. Great fun and much work. Then there was the day when my senior pastor and his teenaged boy landed in the chairs in front of my desk having a shouting match and wanting me to referee or take a side. I was so out of my depth!

I could write pages of these challenges, which I do not consider to be especially grievous, just unique to me. Surely some of you reading this have had far worse difficulties. I only write these as a few examples of the trials that full-time ministry can create. My concern in this chapter is to get this principle in your mind: *the unique trials of ministry are God's assignments for personal AND pastoral growth.*

Those things we often call "problems" at church are hard to resolve, but along the way, they are tools of the Lord to help us mature as pastors. I needed to learn to live and do ministry with very little resources because that first ministry wasn't the last time we had to work with little...AND the *pressure* of small resources caused me to call on God for help and to praise Him in the supply of those needs...AND to learn that I should pursue ministry activity in *faith* believing God would supply what was needed to get His work done. My Senior Pastor was not the last challenging person I worked with in 46 years of ministry! That curmudgeon who didn't want to fund youth parties wasn't the last short-sighted church member I encountered.

Being short of money with babies was just the start of my parenting financial challenges! At a point when my wife and I were in debt and struggling to make ends meet, I reached out to the local representative of a well-known Christian finance ministry. I told him my tale of woe and his response was, "If the church you are in can't pay you enough, you should go to a church that can." Really? Just cut and run for the money? No, God wanted us to stay put, suffer a while longer, then He moved us to a place where eventually He miraculously provided for us abundantly beyond what I could ask or think (Ephesians 3:20). I could have pursued money via finding a larger church that could pay a larger salary, but no church would have done for us what God did in some very unexpected ways. And a larger salary doesn't always make a happier life, just some new trials with the new ministry.

Conclusion

I joined the high school swimming team so I could get in shape for tennis in the spring and learn how to swim well. (I know....) In the middle of my nice plan, the coach walked into practice one day and said with a loud voice, "Lunsford, you and Jones are going to be our butterfliers!" Internally I was incredulous. "You think I am going to represent the team doing the hardest stroke?" Excuse me, but NO. While I could not say "no" out loud, I dragged my feet and eventually was relieved of this duty. What if I had accepted the challenge and tried my hardest to follow the coach's lead? We'll never know because I had not yet learned to accept trials as God's assignments. They were only hardships to be avoided.

God truly has given us "all things we need for life and godliness" but these "things" include the path to possessing Christlike character through the effort of spiritual growth. The man who would be a fruitful pastor must walk on the path embracing the challenges of life and ministry as God's direction toward areas of needed growth.

In the next chapters we will look more deeply at the importance of Christlike character, and we will identify those common issues that most pastors face and some of the ways that a fruitful pastor can grow through them.

Questions/Ideas for Application

Make a list of all the trials in your life currently. Don't be pious and try to minimize them, list them all; personal, relational, pastoral difficulties of all kinds.

Evaluate your responses to these challenges. Which ones are you trying to escape? Which one makes you angry? Which ones make you want to quit?

Consider these difficulties in light of the teaching you have just read. What needs to change in your response to them?

Apply the path of growth from 2 Peter 1:5-7 to your response to these trials. Which steps in the growth process need to be enacted or emphasized to enable your growth in the trials?

Write down a plan for progress in several of these troubling issues.

Act on the plan. Add this plan to your prayer list. Review the plan from time to time. Take joy in the progress and refine the plan as you move forward.

Chapter 9

THE FOUNDATION OF LIFE AND MINISTRY

"I know 17 people who say you are not loving." Gene's[1] statement caught me by surprise and gave me great pause. After all, the shepherd is supposed to love his sheep. While I felt attacked by this man who had generally been a great encourager to me and faithful servant of our church, I did manage to ask a helpful question, "Can you give me a concrete example of something that demonstrates my lack of love?" He replied, "There are times when you walk right past people on Sunday morning without greeting them or shaking their hand." As I considered this observation, I realized that he was right. At that time, I was the worship leader and preacher and responsible to "produce" the morning service. That is, I had to make sure all the moving parts meshed properly which meant I was frequently moving from one place to another and concerned to make sure we started on time and did things well. As I meditated further on his confrontation, I came to realize that I was valuing excellence in the execution of the service over care for the people we were trying to impact. I thanked him for the input and changed both my heart and behavior on Sunday mornings.

Character growth is hard. When I speak of "character," I'm not talking solely about actions. What I mean is putting on the thoughts and motives of Christ that lead to the words and deeds of Christ.[2] Peter called it, "the divine nature" (2 Peter 1:4)

---

[1] A very real person and event but not his real name. And yes…there was more to this story, but the Lord used this critic none-the-less.

[2] I reflect again on Acts 1:1-3 in which Luke asserts that Jesus was with the disciples for 40 days after the resurrection teaching them. Thus, the words

of which we can "partake." The sinful habits of the believer's flesh only depart with great effort. But leave they must if the child of God would honor Christ and obtain the life He intends for us. Even more so, the man who would lead a group of Christians must be an example of what Christlike character looks like, must know how such growth happens, and must be consistently growing in that character so he will lead God's people as God desires.

The pastor's character must grow *consistently*

I remember the day of my ordination examination well. There was a large group of pastors who challenged me to verbalize and defend my understanding of God's truth. They were trying to understand if my theology was orthodox (to their way of understanding the Bible) and if I could adequately explain the Word of God. I remember only one question that stumped me, and it regarded non-Biblical theological reasoning, so I was none the worse for wear. Because I passed the ordination "bar" I felt no need to keep on studying God's Word but have relied solely on the knowledge gained in the years leading up to that defining day.

Is your hair on fire yet? Are you incredulous that I would say such a thing or that anyone might think such a thing? Good. You can rest assured that I have done just the opposite of what I wrote above. I have continued to read and study and receive education, both formal and informal (conferences) because I realized my need of a deepening understanding of God's truth and how to apply it to life and ministry. However, increasing knowledge is not the only attribute in which pastors

---

recorded in the epistles are either the very words of Christ (see Acts 20:35 in which Paul quotes Christ from words we see nowhere in the gospels) or the apostolic rumination of the words of Christ. So, in my definition of Christian character, I assert that when we obey any instruction in the New Testament, we are thinking and/or acting like Christ.

need to be progressing. Pastors also need to be consistently growing in Christlike character.

Every man who serves as a pastor was deemed to be of sufficiently good character according to the standard of 1 Timothy 3:1-7 and Titus 1:5-9 when he was called to his first leadership position. If a man had a glaring weakness, he most likely would not have been considered for the "office of a bishop." Does that positive evaluation mean that he has no need to grow in Christlike character? Or is such an evaluation more equivalent to an ordination exam in that they both establish minimum qualification?

When God established criteria for the selection for men in the pastor/elder/bishop role, it was not meant to be the least common denominator. In my observation, the role of "elder" is a relative position. A young man just out of Bible college might be an "elder" to a group of teens and college-aged students, as I think I was, but that does not mean he is an elder to the entire church. This has been increasingly recognized by churches who may bring a young man on staff but will call him the "director" of a certain ministry until he has proved himself to be called of God as a pastor. The Biblical character qualifications are irreducible minimums which apply to every man who serves as a pastor AND should also be long-range targets for progressive growth.

The Apostle Paul himself cited his need for consistent spiritual growth, even though he was an apostle! After speaking of his past human greatness and his efforts to be more like Christ, Paul says this about his level of spiritual maturity, "Not that I have already attained, or am already perfected; but I press on, that I may lay hold of that for which Christ Jesus has also laid hold of me" (Philippians 3:12). Even though Paul was called and gifted by God and demonstrated godly character, he still had a life-long ambition to be increasingly like Christ.

The New Testament shows us several men who started well but apparently didn't progress consistently. In 2 Timothy

1:15 we read of two men who gave up on the Lord's work, "This you know, that all those in Asia have turned away from me, among whom are Phygellus and Hermogenes." Another man came to different priorities which paused his service to the Lord, "For Demas has forsaken me, having loved this present world" (2 Timothy 4:10). Previously Demas was mentioned quite positively as a co-worker of Paul (Colossians 4:14-15, Philemon 1:24) yet something changed. In Philippians 2:19-21 Paul praised Timothy but lamented that there were so few men willing to go the distance in Christian service with him, "I trust in the Lord Jesus to send Timothy to you shortly, that I also may be encouraged when I know your state. For I have *no one* like-minded, who will sincerely care for your state. For all seek their own, not the things which are of Christ Jesus." These men started well but short-circuited their service for the Lord for what appear to be unspiritual reasons.

Jesus used the image of a shepherd to communicate His commitment to His followers. He noted that in the world of shepherds, there are those who own the sheep and care for them no matter the cost, and there are those who are hired to care for the sheep who will show their heart of self-concern when danger is present, "But a hireling, he who is not the shepherd, the one who does not own the sheep, sees the wolf coming and leaves the sheep and flees; and the wolf catches the sheep and scatters them" (John 10:12). Spiritual shepherds will encounter many kinds of "wolves" from outside the church and from within (Acts 20:29, 3 John 9). When they attack, the local church pastor will have to decide whether he is just there for the paycheck (a "hireling") and as such abandon his post or surrender to the wolves, or if he loves his flock so much that he will grow to meet the challenges. The fruitful pastor aims to grow a little every day and sees the challenges of ministry as special opportunities to grow even more.

The pastor's character requires a *higher aspiration*

The office of spiritual leadership comes with greater demands on a man than that of the average Christian. Some will say, "That's not true," and some will say, "That's not fair," and some will be tempted to give up because they don't think they have what it takes. First, it is true that there is a greater expectation of the pastor than the average Christian. 1 Timothy 3:1-7 says that a man cannot be considered for the pastoral role unless he *already* demonstrates a high level of Christlike character. This is not required of the believer who desires to attach himself to a local church. I realize that all these character traits are targets which God expects of all believers (even the ability to teach the word, according to Hebrews 5:12) but only the pastor must have them in visible measure before he can serve as a spiritual leader, and only the pastor is scrutinized by the entire congregation as to his possession of these qualities when he is called to lead and as he carries out his duties.

Paul's instruction in 1 Corinthians 11:1 sets a very high standard for the spiritual leader when he says, "Imitate me, just as I also imitate Christ." In contemporary terms it has been called, "living in the fishbowl." Some would argue that this truth only applied to the Apostle Paul or perhaps all the Apostles, yet a command for believers to follow the spiritual leader is verbalized in various ways in several passages. Titus 2:7 exhorts the pastor, "In all things showing yourself to be a **pattern** of good works." The command to believers in Hebrews 13:7 makes it quite clear that they are to follow the example of their spiritual leaders, "Remember those who rule over you, who have spoken the word of God to you, **whose faith follow**, considering the outcome of their conduct." 1 Peter 5:3 instructs spiritual leaders (here called "elders") to be **examples** to the flock. I mention again a key verse for spiritual leaders, "Take heed to yourself and to the doctrine. Continue in them, for in doing this you will save both yourself and those who hear you" (1Timothy 4:16).

The spiritual leader does not save himself [3] just by the knowledge of right doctrine, but by the appropriation of that doctrine into life. The fruitful pastor needs to aspire to be like Christ, just as Paul did in Philippians 3. He needs to be constantly progressing and deepening in righteous character so that his people have a growing example to guide them on their journey. He cannot settle for "good enough."

    I began to learn woodworking from a church member who was a high school woodshop teacher. He allowed me to come into his classroom and use the tools while he taught me technique. He told me of his high school shop teacher who pushed the students to do things with excellence. This teacher even advocated for finishing the unseen bottom of a project. His name was "Hess," and the students developed a saying: "do it Hess," as their way of saying to do something with excellence. I'm not sure if my woodworking projects measured up to the "Hess" standard then or now, but I strive to do them well. How much more should we strive for excellence of character as men who lead others to live like Christ?

    The apostle Paul refused to settle for lesser character. In Romans 7 Paul spoke of the struggle he had trying to live like Christ, "For what I am doing, I do not understand. For what I will to do, that I do not practice; but what I hate, that I do" (Romans 7:15). In chapter 8 he spoke of the blessing of knowing that Christ would never abandon him because he had difficulty living righteously. In response to the struggle and God's love this was Paul's commitment, "Do you not know that those who run in a race all run, but one receives the prize? Run in such a way that you may obtain it... (so) I discipline my body and bring it into subjection, lest, when I have preached to others, I myself should become disqualified" (1 Corinthians 9:24, 27). Paul refused to give up on the battle with his flesh for Christlike

---

[3] "Save" seems to be a reference to the preserving of the spiritual life, not the acquiring of it. Philipps, John. *The Pastoral Epistles.* Grand Rapids: Kregal, 2004,138.

character and those of us who lead the body of Christ must do the same. We must not settle at any level of Christlike character but must strive to be more and more like Christ till He calls us home.

Growth in the pastor's character requires a *listening ear*

A "listening ear" is my term derived from the application of two Scriptural principles. The first is the command of personal humility as we read of Christ, "Let nothing be done through selfish ambition or conceit, but in lowliness of mind let each esteem others better than himself. Let this mind be in you which was also in Christ Jesus" (Philippians 2:3, 5). The truth of "lowliness" is more sharply focused on pastors in this familiar passage, "Shepherd the flock of God, which is among you, serving as overseers, not by compulsion but willingly, not for dishonest gain but eagerly; **nor as being lords over those entrusted to you**, but being examples to the flock…Likewise you younger people, submit yourselves to your elders. Yes, **all of you** be submissive to one another, and be **clothed with humility,** for 'God resists the proud, But gives grace to the humble'" (1 Peter 5:2, 3, 5).

The position and role of a spiritual leader in the Body of Christ does not elevate a man beyond the need for Christlike humility. We see the Lord referred to as "gentle and lowly" (humble) (Matthew 11:29) yet somehow pastors gravitate toward the identity of a CEO more than that of a servant. The servant leadership that Jesus modeled and instructed in John 13 is not self-driven or self-affirming but concerned for others. The pastor who is a servant leader will want to be as much like Christ as he can for the purpose of accomplishing Christ's work in Christ's way. If Jesus, in His perfection, didn't elevate Himself to being a domineering leader, then imperfect human pastors must be certain they do not place themselves above others.

This attitude of humility prepares the way for the second Biblical principle which empowers the listening ear, that is, the ministry of the Body of Christ. While the only definition of Christlike conduct is found in the Bible, God not only mediates those truths through the reading and hearing of the Word, but also through personal input. This is a key, but often missing, application of 1 Corinthians 12 which makes it clear that God has given a variety of spiritual gifts to individuals in the Body of Christ for the benefit of the other individuals. 1 Corinthians 12:7, 21, 22 says, "But the manifestation of the Spirit is given to each one for the profit of **all**...and the eye cannot say to the hand, 'I have no need of you'; nor again the head to the feet, 'I have no need of you.' No, much rather, those members of the body which seem to be weaker are necessary." Dare the pastor think that the Biblically aligned encouragement, confrontation, or exhortation which comes from other Christians has no validity? Should he not give prayerful consideration when such words are sincerely spoken to him? Remember, God even spoke to a prophet through a donkey (Numbers 22:28 ff.)!

    Exhibit "A", my confrontation from Gene.[4] I truly thought I loved my congregation, but God saw the need to deepen my love and make it seen more. Another voice that I listened to was at a retreat early in my pastoral journey which featured a keynote speaker who addressed sexual purity in pastors. He spoke at length about the need for pastors to have boundaries like not being alone with a woman, especially in a counseling setting. I was not convinced that all his safeguards were necessary, but I also didn't reject them out of hand. Many years later, I had occasion to meet with a young woman who asked for counsel. The circumstances caused me to feel the need for caution, so my wife was present with me. The woman came for counsel but never came back to church and she privately accused me of impropriety to her grandmother who

---

[4] Later I would see that Gene was doing more than trying to help me. At some time after this when he was acting sinfully and refusing to repent, he tried to discredit me so he might be justified. However, God still spoke some truth through him which I needed to hear in this instance.

was a church member. When I mentioned the presence of my wife, the concern disappeared.

God was speaking through the itinerant teacher who said something I needed to hear just as He has through many people throughout my years of pastoral ministry. I have seen this in my life and that of others in vocational ministry.

- A wise older deacon came to my office to confront me about how I had handled a certain financial appeal. He was right, I had jumped the leadership gun.
- A college-aged young man left our church telling me I was not a gracious leader in his area of ministry.
- A pastor friend of mine ignored exhortations from a church member about his relationship with a certain woman and it led to an affair.
- Another friend ignored the input of his leadership board and was asked to resign.

I could go on with many circumstances, but my point is quite simple: God moves through the Body of Christ so that the members help one another see blind spots, and that includes pastors. Timothy had to be encouraged to not give up in ministry (1 Timothy 1:3). Paul had to exhort believers to accept his definition of maturity (Philippians 3:15). Elders must not act as a "Lord over those entrusted to them" (1 Peter 5:3) but must demonstrate humility along with the entire congregation (1 Peter 5:5) so that God can work through the WHOLE body of believers to help each one grow in Christ as He deems necessary.

The pastor who truly believes in 1 Corinthians 12 will create a collegial atmosphere with the other designated leaders of his church.[5] Even more than the average church member, a pastor should listen to his co-leaders who speak into his life just as he would hope to be welcome to speak into others. The fruitful pastor believes that God will use such men in his life just as He uses them in the lives of other church members. When they come to him, he will not brush aside their concerns.

One of the key voices a pastor ought to listen to is that of his wife. A wife sees and knows more about her husband than anyone else. I'm not advocating for a man to surrender his role of leadership, or for a wife to make herself into the queen Regis of her home and marriage. I am advocating for an application of Ephesians 5:18-21, "And do not be drunk with wine, in which is dissipation; but be filled with the Spirit, speaking to one another in psalms and hymns and spiritual songs, singing and making melody in your heart to the Lord, giving thanks always for all things to God the Father in the name of our Lord Jesus Christ, **submitting to one another** in the fear of God." The truly spiritual husband and wife ought to share godly encouragement back and forth out of a growing relationship with each other in Christ. As such, when a wife shares an observation with her husband like, "You need to talk less in social settings," or "Don't use the term 'old lady' in a sermon," or "I don't think you should spend time with that person," the fruitful pastor will prayerfully consider such input and make changes accordingly, not because his wife is always right, but because she might be acting on the urging of the Holy Spirit out of love for her husband.

I know a man, who is with the Lord now, who was so full of zeal for souls that he inspired other men to aspire to that

---

[5] I don't wish to debate ecclesiology here. I have convictions on how a church ought to be organized and led, which I believe are within the Scriptural boundaries. In my opinion, those boundaries allow for some variation among Bible-believing churches. For this reason, I will sometimes use the term "leader" to designate those men who serve with the vocational pastors.

same thing, but he had no listening ear. He was unable or unwilling to receive any critical input and so made some very public mistakes but steadfastly refused to change his ways even when directly confronted. Those who knew him well humored him, but few looked to him for spiritual guidance. His spiritual immaturity kept him from significant ministry which he deeply desired to do. Good intentions do not trump real maturity fueled by godly input from God's Word AND His people.

The pastor's growth requires *knowledge*

While the growing pastor must assume that God will speak through the Body of Christ, he must also respond to that input wisely. The only source of knowledge about Christlike character is the Bible. I have spoken at length about the need for pastors to be in the Word daily, so I do not intend to repeat myself. What I will emphasize here is the need of the fruitful pastor to gather Bible knowledge to deal with the unique character tests that come through full-time ministry, especially in the form of input from the Body of Christ.

When a pastor encounters opposition to his leadership, debate with his teaching, dissatisfaction with church programs, criticism of his mannerism, or other common difficult ministry-related circumstances, his first response needs to be personal interaction with God and His Word. James 1:19-20 is vital here, "So then, my beloved brethren, let every man be swift to hear, slow to speak, slow to wrath; for the wrath of man does not produce the righteousness of God." A key reason for a pastor to be slow in response to challenges is that he must find a response based in God's truth. This call for truth is part of the path to growth. The fruitful pastor will not assume all input to be equally valid or weighty, nor will he discount it without consideration. Rather the growing pastor will seek God's way in the Word and will discuss what he finds with God in prayer and will arrive at the points of needed change. James 3:12-18, especially vs. 17, should guide his reception of input and his response to it, "The wisdom that is from above is first pure, then peaceable, gentle, willing to yield, full of mercy and good fruits, without partiality and without hypocrisy."

Two responses to challenging input must be avoided: rejecting it outright or accepting it without sufficient consideration. Some men are inclined, perhaps by personality or life experience, to receive all input and attempt adjustments in a misguided effort to keep the peace (in reality just trying to make everyone happy) without prayerful Scriptural consideration. However, some critics are wrong, some are 50% wrong, some are 10% right, while some are on the right track but not completely clear. No matter what the input may be or how hurtful or outlandish it may seem, the fruitful pastor receives it for consideration and seeks God's truth to guide his evaluation of the exhortation and he prayerfully asks God to help him see the needed truth. When change is needed, it must first be at the heart level as that is the real source of our words and deeds (Matthew 15:18) which work out into behavior.

The pastor's growth requires *obedience*

You may feel "a great big 'Duh' coming on" but hold on to it for a minute. The problem of orthodoxy without orthopraxy has been visible since the Lord's brother wrote about it, "Be doers of the word, and not hearers only, deceiving yourselves" (James 1:20). Almost as old as Christianity itself is this exhortation to live out what is known to be right. As with the previous topic of knowledge, I have spoken of this as part of the 2 Peter model of growth, but I mention it again to stress the importance of the pastor's obedience in the process of growth.

A believer cannot grow without the knowledge of what is right and wrong BUT increasing knowledge does not equal greater Christlikeness. Growth only happens through obedience to the truth. Ravi Zacharias, the world-famous apologist, and leader of a ministry that defended God's truth, seemed to have more theological knowledge than most pastors, yet he allowed himself a loophole on obedience in regard to sexual morality. James MacDonald was a widely appreciated preacher and co-authored a book on Biblical Counseling but was forced to resign because of the lack of love in his leadership style. We could go on at length about men both well-known and lesser so, who honored the Lord with their doctrine but not with their actions.

This is a special temptation for pastors who deal in the content of God's Word and care deeply about right theology on a regular basis. There is a subtle mission drift that can happen when pastors begin to think that their superior understanding of orthodox truth is the goal rather than the Christlike character which should result from such knowledge. When a pastor's character fails to match his eloquent expression of God's truth, he can become a reason for people to discount the validity of the Christ life. For the spiritual leader to preach to others about obedience week by week but to not live what he preaches gives credence to the accusation of "hypocrite." Some men will even go beyond accidental hypocrisy to excuse themselves from obedience by asserting, "I give and give in this position; I deserve special privileges—perhaps even the privilege of living above the rules."[6] The article just quoted was written by a pastor who became an adulterer. He writes in an attempt to explain the actions of another pastor who was found to have a hidden life. Leaders can easily offer the same excuses as all disobedient believers when they think or say, "My circumstance is extraordinarily hard," or "Obedience will require too great a sacrifice," or "I'm the leader and that's that for that."

No matter how persuasive the defense is, there is no excuse. God's way must be sought and lived out by the leader who would be fruitful. Of all Christians, the pastoral leader must have a zero tolerance for sin in his life. He must confess the first sin and not live on to spiral into more and greater sin because of his fleshly desires. Even better, he must learn to discern the

---

[6]MacDonald, Gordon. "When Leaders Implode." *Leadership Journal Newsletter*, November 2006: 4.

beginning of temptation and stop the slide toward sin as James said, "Each one is tempted when he is drawn away by his own desires and enticed. *Then*, when desire has conceived, it gives birth to sin; and sin, when it is full-grown, brings forth death" (James 1:14-15).

Many years ago, I heard or read a statement to this effect by John MacArthur, "You can confess your sin in private to God or He will confess it publicly for you."[7] I believe this to be true based on the gracious nature of God and the examples I have observed of men who are caught by others in their sin. The Holy Spirit always nudges our spirit immediately when we do something wrong, and He may do this through other people. If we are tuned in to hear His rebukes, we can confess and make changes before He must use more painful means. In recent years we have watched the public removal of well-known pastors like Mark Driscoll and James MacDonald who both refused lesser confrontations. I have personally seen this in much less notable cases with men who refused to accept the admonitions of their church leadership and make real change based on that input.

Obedience always requires a sacrifice, but it always results in a blessing. God may give some specific blessing, but the most important promised blessings of obedience are the joy and peace of Christ which make the sacrifice worth the effort.

The pastor's growth demonstrates genuine *love for God*

Growing character demonstrates a genuine love for Christ. Supposedly, a man enters vocational ministry because he loves the Lord who saved him and wants others to possess that same relationship. He knows the benefit of the joy and peace and purpose of Christ and wants others to know them also. He appreciates his salvation and wants to help others do the same.

---

[7] I believe I heard it on a radio broadcast. I would cite the exact source if I could!

He loves to worship the Lord corporately because of God's greatness and he longs for his whole congregation to have the same heart. On some level the fruitful pastor is seen to be living out these commands repeated by Jesus, "'You shall love the LORD your God with all your heart, with all your soul, with all your mind, and with all your strength.' This is the first commandment. And the second, like it, is this: 'You shall love your neighbor as yourself.' There is no other commandment greater than these" (Mark 12:30-31). A man who genuinely loves God this way will be growing in Christ. His people will see his progress and follow his example.

Conclusion

A couple of years ago I shot myself in the foot. Not literally, but the impact was quite similar. In order to break a large piece of pressboard before putting it in the garbage bin, I intended to give it a swift blow on the side of the metal dumpster. Sadly, I missed the dumpster, and the wood slipped out of my hands and hit my big toe like it was shot out of a gun. I gave myself an open fracture on my big toe and limped for weeks. I wish I had been more careful.

Allowing sin to remain has a much greater consequence than my poorly executed demolition did. It truly is shooting yourself in the foot *on purpose.* If an injured foot results in a physical limp, a sinful life will surely result in a spiritual limp or even become incapacitating. How can a pastor expect to accomplish God's will in God's way while He refuses God's instruction about his life? The fruitful pastor will do the hard work with God as soon as it is needed and will walk in step with God as he seeks to care for His sheep. In the next chapter we will examine specific character challenges every pastor will have to deal with at some point.

Chapter 10

CRUCIAL ASPECTS OF CHARACTER

When I was a young teenager, we lived next to a family with three girls, the youngest of which was about 5 years old. Often in the summer I would swim in their above-ground pool and "hang out" with them. One day we were playing some backyard baseball, and because the 5-year-old was so small I put my arms around her and helped her swing the plastic bat. We were having a great time until their miniature pug dog thought I was harming his girl and latched on to the back of my upper arm. I immediately cried out in pain, stood up and was shocked to see him hanging on my arm. I shook him off, ran and vaulted the short fence to the safety of my yard. The dog left a perfect circular imprint of ALL his teeth on my arm and a life-long caution around all dogs. Previously, I had no concern about that dog. I had been around it, petted it, and never had a reason to think that it might hurt me. Why would I need to be cautious around a small dog with whom I was familiar? I discovered that my pre-conceptions were wrong. Neither size nor familiarity with a dog removes danger.

A lifetime devoted to full-time ministry is a wonderful career choice that is expected to be full of blessing and fulfillment, but it also possesses unexpected risks. Some of them are issues common to all Christians and some are unique to those in vocational ministry. These potential problems can sneak up on a pastor and bite him, leaving a mark which is hurtful, and can be debilitating or even ministry-ending. Some of these challenges are obvious and others are not. In this chapter I will touch on a series of crucial issues about which every pastor should exercise special caution to be growing through not falling into.

Personal impediment

"Your way of thinking is completely natural for you." Rarely am I able to quote a preacher or his sermon, but this phrase from a friend who spoke in my church burned its way into my mind because of its humorously profound validity. Every human being grows up in a family, a geographic location, a culture, and has various experiences and receives some kind of education. All these and more combine with basic inborn personality proclivities[1] to produce their unique way of understanding themselves and the world around them. Generally, each person believes that their way of thinking and living is normal and thus should be acceptable to those around them. This belief is encouraged by the American notion that we are endowed by God with the "right to life, liberty, and the pursuit of happiness" as stated in the preamble to the Declaration of Independence. Men who take this way of thinking about life into vocational ministry are destined to find themselves in conflict with members of their congregations who hold the same opinion about their own way of thinking.

God calls all believers to a standard of living that is higher than "normal," that is to be like Christ. This is especially important to those who would be spiritual leaders of congregations. "Let us lay aside every **weight**, and the **sin** which so easily ensnares us, and let us run with endurance the race that is set before us" (Hebrews 12:1). The word "weight," only used in this verse in the New Testament, has a root definition of, "a burden [*as in something heavy*], a weight, encumbrance."[2] The next words in the verse, "and the sin" tell us that a weight is not a

---

[1] There is no authoritative declaration of how the thing we call "personality" is affected by genetics. My purely anecdotal take has been formed by the experience of having twin girls who, although coming from the same parents and life circumstances, had significant uniqueness from their earliest days till now, 40+ years later.

[2] Thayer, Joseph Henry. *Thayer's Greek English Lexicon of the New Testatment.* Grand Rapids, Michigan: Zondervan , 1974, 437.

sin but is something that slows the believer as he runs the race of the Christian life and service. "In application the author probably has in mind those hindrances which may not be sinful in themselves, but which would prevent the progress that ought to occur."[3]

Before I attempt to enumerate what some of these "weights" might be for pastors, I want to make it clear that I am in no way trying to establish a list of dos and don'ts outside Scripture. I agree with Bruce, "It may well be that what is a hindrance to one entrant in this spiritual contest is not a hindrance to another; each must learn for himself what in this case is a weight or impediment."[4] Having said that, I do find in the Scripture very challenging instructions regarding how we live life and do ministry.

One of the prime aspects of ministry that can be a "weight" which impedes pastoral fruitfulness is the need for **cultural adaptation**. The apostle Paul is our prime example of personal flexibility motivated by the Great Commission:

> For though I am free from all men, I have made myself a servant to all, that I might win the more; and to the Jews I became as a Jew, that I might win Jews; to those who are under the law, as under the law, that I might win those who are under the law; to those who are without law, as without law (not being without law toward God, but under law toward Christ), that I might win those who are without law; to the weak I became as weak, that I might win the weak. I have become all things to all men, that I might by all means save some. Now this I do for the

---

[3]Kent, Homer A. *The Epistle to the Hebrews.* Grand Rapids: Baker Book House, 1972, 257.
[4]Bruce, F. F. *The Epistle to the Hebrews.* Grand Rapids: Wm B. Eerdmans, 1990, 336.

gospel's sake, that I may be partaker of it with you. (1 Corinthians 9:19-23)

"Culture" is a broad word that touches every aspect of life and includes God's commands for those who call themselves "Christian." The foods we eat, the clothes we wear, the house we live in, and the way we interact with people, the music we love, and more are all part of our "culture." The apostle Paul was willing to leave the Pharisee culture in which he was raised and embrace a Greek way of life—then to put it back on—and off—and move in other directions so his audience would be comfortable enough with him to listen to the message he preached. When we send missionaries to foreign lands, we expect them to adapt to the culture. One of my friends who serves in a land very different from our own said this in all sincerity, "The Muslims don't eat pork, and the Hindus don't eat beef, so we eat a lot of chicken." We admire his sacrifice but assume that in America we are all the same, so no adaptation is necessary.

What kind of cultural shifts might we need to make as church leaders in the USA? I will share **a few changes I have made** ONLY as examples to challenge your thinking about your situation. I gave up wearing ties (and later suits/sport coats) because I began to look closely at the people in the congregation AND those who I hoped would come (unbelievers and wayward believers). I realized that my business attire[5] might cause them to feel under-dressed. I didn't want that distraction, so I softened my dress style while still being more "dressed-up" than most of the people in my congregations.

I have consistently moved my churches toward music that seems accessible to the average Christian AND the unbeliever who might come to church (save your stones—we always sang hymns as part of our worship also). We all have

---

[5]I was raised by an old-school pastor who also worked in men's clothing stores. I know how to tie a tie and wear a suit…and I like dressing up!

personal preferences, but we cannot impose those on our flocks. We need to find what enables their worship. I have adapted my vocabulary over the years to respond to input from the congregation and my wife! I have worked at sermon preparation with a view to how my words will be received, not just what I think is the most eloquent or enjoyable way to say something.

Excellence is a flexible factor of culture. I have been in churches that reach the upwardly mobile and those who reach the "least of these" and every degree in-between. There are many ways to do church, but we must consider whether our level of excellence matches our community. This is something for a pastor to consider personally as well as to lead his church toward. Proverbs 22:29 states an important principle, "Do you see a man who excels in his work? He will stand before kings; He will not stand before unknown men." I heard a foreign missionary say that they aimed their ministry at the top level of society, because in that culture, the top could reach down to those below, but those below could not reach up. Our tendency with excellence often is to look at our present condition and say, "Well...that's just who we are" or "that's the best we can do," without stopping to ask, who should we be if we are going to reach our community?

A third "weight" that can hinder fruitfulness in ministry is what I'd like to call the **stuff of life**. In 2 Timothy 2:4 we read, "No one engaged in warfare entangles himself with the affairs of this life, that he may please him who enlisted him as a soldier." We all must eat, and sleep, and care for our family, and prepare for retirement, etc. My pastor-father never wanted to own a home because that would tie him down to a community and he wouldn't be able to leave one church for another easily. While I do not agree with that thinking (and I do own a house), it is possible to have such an attachment to owning a home that a pastor will make choices like living far from his church or getting a second job to afford a bigger home. The question we must ask is, does my home help or hinder the ministry to which God has called me?

My first wife, who worked full-time, came up with an idea for a store that she and one of our daughters could operate. I thought better of it and told her so but let her follow her dream. We put many hours and dollars into the effort which we did not have to give. We beat that horse till we sold it and took a loss. God was gracious to make up for the financial loss in an unexpected way, but the time and fatigue could not be replaced. It was a weight we did not need.

In one of my churches, I served as a chaplain for several first responder organizations. At one point my leadership said that I was doing too much outside the church and I had to let something go, which I did. There was nothing wrong with any of my involvements, but they were keeping me from my top priority.

I've known men who were fanatical about exercise or a certain diet which was a preference but not a medical necessity. Some men, like me, must consider whether food itself is creating weight that slows us down in life and ministry. Some men carry their golf clubs and some their fishing pole wherever they go. There is nothing wrong with a hobby unless it becomes so important that it interferes with ministry. I have no desire to criticize any personal enjoyment or to create a list of "approved" vices. Rather, I only want to challenge you to examine your lifestyle as to its impact on your fruitfulness in ministry.

The last weight I would like to consider is a very subjective broad topic I'll call **personal style**. This is a combination of maturity, personality, methodology, and a man's notion of what is normal (see the discussion above on "natural thinking"). A missionary said to me about his home church, "If anyone but [name of his pastor] was pastoring that church, there would be 200 people in it" (which would make it substantially larger than it persisted in being). Eventually, that pastor resigned and migrated to a secular career although he stayed a fervent

Christian who was loud, gregarious, and hyper-passionate to a fault. When I was leaving a chaplaincy I directed, due to moving away, the Chief said to me, "We need to find someone with the right personality. I don't know about his [another evangelical pastor who served as a chaplain] relationship with the troops or his counseling of them, but he's brash and overly outspoken." Both men had (and still have!) a heart for people but their personal uniqueness kept them from more fruitful ministry.

Some men are so introverted that they do not speak up or lead. Some are so boisterous that no one will attempt to speak back to them. It has taken me years—decades even—to become more sensitive to others when I am in a discussion, and I'm sure I still do not always notice when I ride over others. I tried to help a pastor who was eventually fired in part (there were more issues!) because he was chronically late—to virtually everything. His people even coined a phrase, "Joe time" (not his real name). I realize that God uses different men in different cultures, but that doesn't mean that pastors should *assume* that all their ways are normal and without need for adaptation. "We often hear, alas, the question: what is the harm or the sin in my doing this or that thing; engaging in this business, or indulging in that pleasure? The question is answered here; is the thing a **weight,** or is it a **wing**? Is it that which speeds you on your course or does it hold you back? Weights are not necessarily external: they are first of all in the heart. Duties are never weights. But the moment a thing gets a place in my heart and mind which is not in God's mind for me, it becomes a weight, no matter what it is."[6]

A mature believer readily gives up something that is a hindrance to fruitful ministry. "If we would travel far, **we must travel light.** There is in life the essential duty of discarding things. There may be habits, pleasures, self-indulgences, associations

---

[6]Newell, William R. *Hebrews Verse by Verse.* Chicago: Moody Press, 1947, 400.

which hold us back. We must shed them as the athlete sheds his track suit when he goes to the starting mark."[7]

Trivializing sin

I realize that to write such a title in a book for pastors is to risk insulting them, but I have dealt with too many men who are not in ministry anymore, and some who are there but should not be, to think this an unnecessary reminder. Hebrews 12:1 says that not only must we lay aside good/neutral things (weights) that hinder us in our service to God, but we must also lay aside sin which "ensnares" (NKJV), or "entangles" (NIV, NASB). The Greek word for "ensnare" ("beset" KJV) is only used here in the New Testament and has a literal raw meaning of "to stand around"[8] or "clings so closely."[9] The idea is that sin quickly takes up residence in our life. Kent explains, "The reference is probably not to some specific sin, but to the peculiar characteristic of all sin as continually surrounding men and so easily getting hold of them."[10] One of the earliest teachings on sin illustrates this principle clearly, "If you do well, will you not be accepted? And if you do not do well, sin lies at the door. And its desire is for you, but you should rule over it" (Genesis 4:7). When God spoke to Cain about his anger with his brother, he exhorted him to shut the door on temptation. Cain chose to open the door, and things went downhill from there.

Pastors regularly expound on living the Christian life with its God-commanded virtues and condemned vices. We lament those who fall away from the Lord for adultery, drunkenness, or even disbelief. We extoll the virtues of honesty,

---

[7]Barclay, William. *The letter to the Hebrews*. Philadelphia: Westminster Press, 1976, 173.
[8]Kent, Homer A. *The Epistle to the Hebrews*. Grand Rapids: Baker Book House, 1972, 258.
[9]Hewitt, Thomas. *The Epistle to the Hebrews*. Grand Rapids: Wm B. Erdmans, 1976, 190.
[10]Ibid., Kent, 258.

generosity, and all the virtuous qualities of Christ. Yet we may fall prey to a failure to robustly examine our own life for sins that we might not think are significant. In an article by Randy Alcorn in his online magazine, he wrote about Pastor John Piper who after many years of ministry took an extended time out to evaluate his life, and after eight months came back from his self-imposed spiritual sabbatical with this statement, "As I tried to be very specific in identifying my characteristic sins, it became evident what they were — namely, an ugly cluster of selfishness, anger, self-pity, quickness to blame, and sullenness."[11] If a man desires to be fruitful for the Lord throughout his God-given years of ministry, he must honestly look in the mirror of God's Word (James 1:23-25) and give due attention to every blemish of sin the mirror reveals. There can be no such thing as an insignificant sin because ALL sin wants to "stand around," that is, it to remain and multiply.

One of the reasons sins are overlooked by those in vocational ministry is the temptation of substituting skill or success for righteousness. In a dinner conversation which included discussing a mutual acquaintance who was overcome with homosexual sin while he worked on a church staff, someone commented that often highly gifted people have a weakness which must be overlooked because of the great value of the gifted ability. A pastor friend served in a setting where he was personally acquainted with Mark Driscoll, the former pastor of megachurch Mars Hill, in the Seattle area. Sometime after Driscoll's pastoral failure, my friend said this in a conference workshop, "Mark Driscoll possessed all the qualities of 1 Timothy 3 except two." Mars Hill exploded from zero to thousands of worshippers on multiple campuses in 10 years, all during which Pastor Driscoll's harsh ways were hurting his colleagues. He failed to listen to the kind rebukes and eventually

---

[11] Alcorn, Randy. *Eternal Perspectives Ministries.* October 31, 2024, https://www.epm.org/blog/2018/Oct/12/piper-identifying-fighting-besetting-sins.

was forced to resign, and the entire Mars Hill experiment deflated and hurt many people in the process. Neither ability nor success compensate for a lack of righteousness. We must not think that giftedness balances wickedness. The fruitful pastor tries to honestly see himself before the Lord and workday by day toward a whole Christlike character.

Family life

Jesus said these words that must have shocked His clan-living hearers even more than they do us today, "He who loves father or mother more than Me is not worthy of Me. And he who loves son or daughter more than Me is not worthy of Me" (Matthew 10:37), and "Then He said to another, 'Follow Me.' But he said, 'Lord, let me first go and bury my father.' Jesus said to him, 'Let the dead bury their own dead, but you go and preach the kingdom of God'" (Luke 9:59-60). Did Jesus mean that a man who would truly follow Christ, especially one who serves as a pastor, must leave his family of origin completely? Other Scripture would argue against that interpretation (i.e., John 19:27, 1 Timothy 3:5, 1 Timothy 5:8). Rather, Christ is asserting that obedience to Him must be above all. What does this look like for a pastor in a local church?

These instructions from Christ are broad principles that must be contemplated, integrated with other Scripture, evaluated, and applied by every Christian. In this, pastors are no different than the men in their churches. However, there is a unique aspect to the pastor's "job" in that he is paid to "work for God." He is helping people know Christ and live godly lives. How can a man turn away from those in spiritual need "just" to play catch with his budding Little Leaguer? Or, given the importance of family (1 Timothy 3:4, Titus 1:6) how can he not spend quality time with his children? How can a pastor block out a night to take his wife to dinner when someone's marriage is on the brink of ruin? At one point in my ministry life, how can a man get up in the middle of the night to serve people in the community as a police chaplain and come home too tired to serve the family? Or, also in my case, how can a man set aside every Friday afternoon and evening to help with his son's high school football team when there are sinners to be won and sermons to be written?

Every pastor must wrestle with the needs, opportunities, demands, and expectations of ministry versus the needs and expectations of his wife and children. How can a man choose between two such important priorities? First, he must remember that there is only one husband/father in his home. No one else can take his place. No one else will love his wife and train his children if he does not. When the years at home with children are passed, the opportunities to build relationships and nurture their walk with God will be greatly diminished. The fruitful pastor must also remember that he is not the key member of the church. Yes, he is the key leader, but as such, he should be training the church members to minister to one another and to depend on God themselves. He must guard against becoming their leaning post in place of God. As such, his refusal to be everywhere all the time with everyone will be helpful to their spiritual development.

The fruitful pastor must be proactive in considering his schedule in ministry and the needs of his home. Not every request for ministry must rise to the top of the "to-do" list immediately. Pastors are one of the few professionals (I use the word cautiously) who are expected (often implied but not spoken out loud) to be on call 24/7 for their people. I had a decades-long acquaintance with a pastor who was extremely successful yet died alone and in obscurity, estranged from his family. One of his key failures was always making the church the top priority in his use of his time. *There is no quality time without quantity time.* While he would say he loved his wife and children, they always took a back seat to the ministry. Eventually his wife grew tired of it and initiated a separation which led to divorce.[12] Their relationship deteriorated because he didn't listen ("listening ear!"), and he soon found solace in the arms of another woman. His life and ministry devolved from there.

As Bible college students, my friends and I discussed the need for this balance of life and ministry. I concluded (my conviction, not one I am promoting as absolute for you) that for the first 20 years of ministry, my time priority choices would "lean" toward the family, and in my second 20 years my time priority choices would "lean" more toward the ministry. That doesn't mean I was always at home in the evening with my family or that I never had to say "no" to my children about my time or our activities. And it in no way means I neglected my wife in the "empty nest" years. It does mean that I let Christ be responsible for the church by consistently giving thoughtful attention to my time priorities for home and ministry.

God's servants are called on to make sacrifices for His work. Jesus made it clear in various ways that one who truly follows Him must be *willing* to sacrifice wealth (Mark 10:21), family (Luke 14:26), houses and lands (Mark 10:29), even his own life (John 12:25). Yet at the same time the faithful pastor is called on to love and provide for his family. How each pastor will find God's path among these various priorities will be unique. He cannot embrace either the ministry or the family to the exclusion of the other. One of the vital reasons to spend time interacting with God through His Word and prayer each morning is to constantly seek His promptings through the Holy Spirit to guide the choices he makes as he cares for family and flock.

---

[12] I have seen this pattern many times when a Christian marriage is in crisis. The husband has been deficient in some way for years and the wife submits in a mistaken understanding of scripture (Ephesians 5:23), until she decides not to take it anymore. She initiates separation in some form and appears to be the sinner in the situation, and she is, but the real origin of the problem is the husband and their joint lack of marriage growth.

I spoke with a man who did not get this balance right and whose ministry life came to an end after being caught in sin. His family mistakenly played into the problem. When he walked in the door in the evening sometimes he would be on the phone in a pastoral conversation. "Don't bother daddy, he's doing important things," his wife would say to the children. He had bought into the mistaken notion of feeling personal esteem by being often sought for pastoral help. His sense of importance in that identity came to rule his life. Eventually, his family grew tired of their husband and father's preoccupation and home life became more burden than blessing to him. He sought a friend in other places...and the story ended in heartbreak, disgrace, resignation, and a new career.

Sexual integrity

"Integrity is the practice of being honest and showing a consistent and uncompromising adherence to strong moral and ethical principles and values."[13] The New Testament word "purity" is from the same root word as "holy" and means, "to be pure from defilement, not contaminated."[14] The man who practices sexual integrity has a zero tolerance for impurity or defilement. He strives for his behavior to be wholly proper regarding God's will for his sexuality. That will is stated in Hebrews 13:4, "Marriage is honorable among all, and the bed undefiled; but fornicators and adulterers God will judge." In other words, there is one and only one proper place for sexual activity, inside his marriage.

The godly pastor does not have sexual contact of any sort (regardless of Bill Clinton's statement attempting to change the definition of sex) with anyone other than his wife. There is

---

[13] From the Oxford Living Dictionary published by Oxford Press and quoted in Wikipedia.
[14] Vine, W. E. *Vine's Expository Dictionary of Biblical Words.* Nashville, TN: Thomas Nelson, 1985, 498.

no justification for any kind of touching, kissing, or sexual activity of any kind at all, period. Full stop. The godly pastor simply draws a line in the sand and such temptation is dealt with before God, so it is never a thought entertained, or an action completed. When temptations arise, he turns from them. If they progress to the level of contemplated sinful thinking, he confesses them and creates a plan to stop the temptation at the first thought the next time. He doesn't wait till the temptation has given birth to sin (James 1:14-15). I am not advocating for a "don't ever touch anyone at all" standard. We commonly shake hands to greet people, we hug those who appreciate or desire a more personal connection and with a few we are particularly fond of—both men and women, and we have appropriate physical interaction with our families. But none of this is flirtatious, romantic, or sexual in its motive or execution.

The godly pastor does not flirt.[15] He doesn't curry the favor of women to whom he might be attracted. If he senses someone flirting with him, he takes appropriate steps to curtail such behavior. Flirting is an active part of expressing attraction and interest in the process of finding a mate (or in today's world, a casual sexual partner!) In marriage, flirting is part of initiating physical intimacy. While the world may call such behavior harmless,[16] it is a first step on the path to a place the godly pastor must not go with anyone but his wife. 1 Timothy 5:1 reinforces this standard of behavior when it says that a pastor is to treat older women as mothers and younger (women) as sisters, with all purity. The pastor is expressly instructed to be an example in purity, "Let no one despise your youth, but be an example to the

---

[15] I will not make all my comments gender inclusive, but the principles would apply equally to men if a pastor was tempted to have relational or sexual thoughts about men. I am personally aware of several pastors who failed out of ministry for this very reason, but I will focus on the more common problem in the way I verbalize things.

[16] In recent years unwanted flirting has also fallen out of favor in the secular world. It is commonly seen as part of the process of attempting to create a sexual contact when it may not be wanted.

believers in word, in conduct, in love, in spirit, in faith, in purity" (1 Timothy 4:12). You cannot be half pure! A dirty hand needs cleaning no matter how much of the skin is covered with muck. Sexual integrity must be whole to exist at all.

In one of my ministries, we were preparing to hire an administrative assistant, and our board chairman came to discuss it. His wife told him that we should not hire a certain woman in the church (who was the kind of involved lay person we would have considered). When he asked her why, she said, "Do you see how she looks at the pastor?" Apparently, his wife noticed something dangerous in that woman's appreciation of me. I immediately agreed with him and his wife, believing that God was directing (see listening ear in chapter 7). We hired another woman, who became a great team member, and there was no sin or temptation!

The godly pastor does not look at pornography. If Jesus' command in Matthew 5:28 ("whoever looks at a woman to lust for her has already committed adultery with her in his heart") is not sufficient to establish this standard, then perhaps this broad command will be helpful in identifying right and wrong, "Finally, brethren, whatever things are true, whatever things are **noble**, whatever things are just, whatever things are **pure**, whatever things are lovely, whatever things are of good report, if there is any **virtue** and if there is anything praiseworthy—meditate on these things" (Philippians 4:8). No lie of the flesh can justify this behavior that is often viewed as adultery by the wife of the man who partakes. No amount of stress relief justifies this behavior which is a double sin—both sexual sin and a failure to seek God's help through prayer for anxiety.

Why is sexual sin such a danger for a pastor? While every man and woman are unique, and every sinful choice has unique elements, there are commonalities among men in vocational ministry who fall into sexual immorality. Foremost among these contributing factors is the position of a pastor. He is a designated leader which in some eyes makes him important.

If he is good at ministry, he is spiritually mature and thought to be a somewhat "ideal" man by many. If he is a good pastor, he is compassionate. If he counsels women alone and demonstrates that compassion and maturity, he becomes highly desirable to a woman who may be treated poorly by the man in her life. This motivates such a woman to pursue her pastor.

Another factor that leads to sexual sin is the condition of the pastor's own marriage and family. If he has not balanced life and ministry well, he may be experiencing unhappiness in the very place that should be encouraging him. In such discomfort, a man may embrace someone or something (pornography) that makes him feel better.

In Proverbs 7:26 we read of the impact of an immoral woman in these words, "She has cast down many wounded, and all who were slain by her were **strong men**." We like to see ourselves as strong men, but God says that sin is stronger. That's why we are to run from it—not indulge it and then try to manage it (1 Timothy 6:11).

Honesty

Many years ago, I had a Christian friend who went to work as an assistant prosecuting attorney. His assigned area was fraud, and he said that most of his cases were based in church settings. What an awful reality and reputation! Men in positions of elevated respect, like the pastorate, face several temptations in regard to honesty. One that seems to be on the rise in recent years (or does the internet just make it more discoverable?) is **plagiarism**. Recently a man in our network was asked if he was preaching the sermons of a certain well-known celebrity preacher. His response was to resign.

A simple Google search for the words, "pastor fraud," turns up many headlines like this, "Californian pastor gets 24 years in prison for defrauding...." "Pastor will plead guilty in $33M investment scheme...." I've personally known of **leaders who took advantage of church members** in one way or another including investments in diamonds, or a "Christian" bank, or soliciting pre-payments for funeral services, then leaving the church before members could collect. Much more common is the misuse of church funds, whether out of the desperation of debt or some malicious motive. It is quite common for embezzling to begin with "borrowing" money for some short-term need or want. Such borrowing easily gets out of control and the only way back is to confess and make restitution, which usually leads to the loss of a job. Whether these were well-intended plans that went bad, I don't know. But I know they were self-serving from the start and not part of the ministry Christ has commanded for His undershepherds. Better not to start. Best to humble yourself and ask for financial help when it is needed.

Honesty can be an issue in the **use of work time**. The average pastor of the average church has little to no staff and he is alone in the office or, quite commonly now, working from home or a favorite coffee shop. These circumstances make it possible for a pastor to work less than the expected hours either on purpose or by accident. Pastors with a large staff have some built-in accountability, yet not even they have a boss looking over their shoulder. The fruitful pastor must give due consideration to how he uses his time as a steward of his job and the people over whom God has placed him.

The **call to vocational ministry** might seem like an odd issue to consider under honesty, but it bears consideration. Simply put, pastors should be genuinely committed to where they are and what they are supposed to be doing. I realize that we must pursue God's call to a specific place and role, but there can be temptation to seek a job for a paycheck. This can happen when a man is first trying to enter vocational ministry, or as a result of the unexpected hard ending of a pastorate. It can also happen after being in a church for some time and coming to a place of discontent. The fruitful pastor needs to be honest with God about his concerns and desires in his place of ministry. The unease might be from God, as I have experienced on several occasions before a ministry transition, or it might also be from a sinful desire for more money or significance or ease. At some point, to continue serving a church without a committed heart is dishonest and needs to be dealt with for the sake of the pastor, his family, and the church.

Ministry jealousy

"You know about the competition..." a friend said to me, as he elaborated about certain men who were always comparing the size and significance of their church ministries. This was no speculation, as he was in a position to know. I should hardly need to mention the relevant scripture, but this is a prime example of what is wrong with such rivalry, "Let nothing be done through selfish ambition or conceit, but in lowliness of mind let each esteem others better than himself" (Philippians 2:3). Jealousy is a strong motivator but a sinful basis for God's work. The godly pastor must check his heart regularly to be certain that he is focused on making more disciples of Christ, and not just trying to claim a larger attendance.

The reason this is especially tempting for pastors is our human nature which tends toward pride. Our natural condition is laid out in stark reality in this passage, "The works of the flesh are evident, which are: adultery, fornication, uncleanness, lewdness, idolatry, sorcery, hatred, contentions, **jealousies**, outbursts of wrath, **selfish ambitions**, dissensions, heresies, **envy**, murders, drunkenness, revelries" (Galatians 5:19-21). I realize that at salvation the power of sin is broken, and the Christian is given a new nature, but the pull of the flesh dies hard. It is completely natural for men to want to brag about "their" accomplishment in building anything, even the Body of Christ, but they must deal with this temptation just as surely as they would any other.

Leadership impatience

Impatience in the Lord's work is a character issue that seems quite unimportant compared to such heavy weights as sexual immorality or honesty. Perhaps the significance is that it afflicts so many pastors and is not perceived as a defect of character. All churches (and other ministries a man of God might lead) need to make steps of progress. A good pastor should be looking down the road and finding needed improvements and guiding his people toward them. The problem, in my observation, is this—most men have good vision but some stumble over the obstacle of timing.

There are multiple commands to those in spiritual leadership to be patient. I will only cite 2 Timothy 2:24, "A servant of the Lord must not quarrel but be gentle to all, able to teach, patient." God commands patience in leadership with individuals and with the whole local church. None of us know the mind of the Lord outside the truth of the Bible. We don't know how He is working in a person or an organization. We don't know if or when a new building is needed. We don't know if or when a new staff member should be brought to the team. We don't know if or when _____ (fill in the blank) is needed in a particular ministry. I will talk more about the ways and means of ministry leadership in a subsequent chapter, but for now, what every pastor needs to consider is whether he is approaching ministry decisions with patience.

Why is this so dangerous for the spiritual leader? Because there is a temptation for a pastor to see any obstacle to his vision for progress as ungodly. Those on his leadership team who might not agree with his vision, timing, or methodology can be seen as trying to usurp his leadership. Such a pastor may believe that progress must be made and those who stand in the way are at fault. This attitude was summarized well by one pastor who was mandated by his church to get counseling, "If people would do what I ask them to the first time, I would not get upset."[17] The fruitful pastor rests in godly methods of leadership bathed in prayer and carried out while resting in God.

How can a pastor avoid these dangers?

Vigilance

Accept this warning along with those you may have heard elsewhere. How often have you quoted this verse or heard someone else quote it, "Pride goes before destruction, And a haughty spirit before a fall" (Proverbs 16:18)? You are probably just as familiar with this line from 1 Corinthians 10:12, "Let him who thinks he stands take heed lest he fall." Maybe these lesser-known observations by Solomon will help you, "Do not correct a scoffer, lest he hate you; Rebuke a wise man, and he will love you. Give instruction to a wise man, and he will be still wiser; Teach a just man, and he will increase in learning" (Proverbs 9:8-9). God has brought you here in this book at this moment for a reason. In our ministry network, the last four men who fell out of the pastorate due to sin (of various kinds) were on the board at one time or another where I served as Executive Director. On multiple occasions I said to my men, "I'm here for you, ask for help," but they waited till the plane was just about to hit the water, or had already crashed, before calling for help.

Growth

Go back to the earlier chapters based on 2 Peter 1:1-11 and use the process of growth to mature through the particular dangers which are tempting you. Proactively build righteousness. Do not wait for temptations to turn into sin and sin to turn into bad character and bad character to bring the downfall of your ministry.

---

[17]McKenzie, Michael. *Don't Blow Up Your Ministry.* Downers Grove, IL: Intervarsity Press, 2021, 98.

Conclusion

I recently attended a "living memorial" service for a pastor who will soon be in heaven. He has served faithfully in the pastorate and other ministries and was suddenly given a terminal diagnosis. He was particularly keen to have this event so he could exhort his family and friends to faith in Christ and service for Him. His family, long term friends, pastors of his local church and current and former coworkers all spoke of their love and admiration for this genuine servant of God. His wife quoted these familiar verses, "I have fought the good fight, I have finished the race, I have kept the faith. Finally, there is laid up for me the crown of righteousness, which the Lord, the righteous Judge, will give to me on that Day, and not to me only but also to all who have loved His appearing" (2 Timothy 4:7-8).

How does a man make it to his seventh decade with joy in his heart having had a fruitful blessed life and ministry, and appreciation from at least the several hundred people who gathered to show their love for him? In contrast, one could ask, why do many pastors *not make it* to such a wonderful point in life?[18] I would suggest that it is because they failed to heed these words sent by the Apostle Paul to pastor Timothy, "But in a great house there are not only vessels of gold and silver, but also of wood and clay, some for honor and some for dishonor. Therefore, if anyone cleanses himself from the latter, he will be a vessel for honor, **sanctified** and useful for the Master, prepared for every good work" (2 Timothy 2:20-21). The pastor who would complete his days of ministry in the joy of Christ with which he began will only do so by promptly dealing with the challenges of life and ministry in a godly way. In saying this I am not pointing a finger at pastors as inherently flawed (after all, I am one!), rather I am pointing out the dangerous nature of the position of vocational spiritual leadership. The fruitful pastor

---

[18]In a quick review I can count 17 men who have left the ministry due to sin over 40 years in our network, which had 100 churches at one time and now has 65.

faces these dangers with a determination to grow in Christ through the challenges and he consistently moves more toward his destiny of Christlike perfection.

Introduction to Section 2

GROWING IN THE WORK OF A SPIRITUAL LEADER

The qualification for being a spiritual leader in the Body of Christ is expressed in the word "elder" while the work is defined by two terms, shepherding, and overseeing (1 Peter 5:2). To be a shepherd, in the time when the Bible was written, was to be responsible for the productive care of a flock of sheep. Psalm 23 uses that imagery to illustrate our relationship with God, Who provides sustenance, guidance, peace, and protection, with the goal of eternal life with Himself. The New Testament pastor (a translation of the word "shepherd" when used to refer to a spiritual leader in a church) is a channel of God's care, and in conjunction with the Holy Spirit's empowerment, he is a key spiritual leader in the lives of those entrusted to him by the Chief Shepherd (1 Peter 5:4) leading them on to their eternal life with Him.

The job of shepherding included leadership (Psalm 23, "he leads me..."). The role of spiritual leader in the church reflects this picture in the instruction which uses the words "shepherd" and "overseer" together in one sentence (1 Peter 5:2). Shepherding emphasizes the care of the sheep as individuals, while the term "overseer" is focused more on the flock (church) as a whole. No doubt Peter had the personal exhortation of Jesus in mind, to "feed (shepherd[19]) His sheep" (John 21:17), as he penned these words.

---

[19] The word means, "to feed or tend a flock of sheep, to keep sheep." Thayer, Joseph Henry. *Thayer's Greek English Lexicon of the New Testament.* Grand Rapids, Michigan: Zondervan, 1974, 527.

The phrase "pastors and teachers" (Ephesians 4:11) which most scholars believe would better be understood as a hyphenated term "pastor-teacher,"[20] causes us to understand that the Word of God is the key tool to be used by the spiritual shepherd in both feeding and leading God's people. Just as the feeding of the literal sheep isn't the goal of the earthly shepherd, so too the communication of God's Word is not the goal of pastoring, rather it is the means to the goal of reaching the "other sheep" (those not yet born again, John 10:16) and nurturing believers to maturity (Ephesians 4:13). This dovetails with Jesus' command of a fruitful Christian life (John 15). The fruitful pastor is the one who is caring for God's flock in such a way that they are healthy, reproducing sheep who bring honor to their Savior/owner.

Some pastors would like to divorce the work of the shepherd from that of the overseer. They prefer the ministry of teaching the Word to that of leading God's flock. God's Word shows no such dichotomy; rather, the two aspects of ministry are inseparably linked so that teaching is leading and leading is teaching if they are done as God intended. Having said that, I fully affirm God's instruction of 1Timothy 5:17 which allows for some spiritual leaders to focus their activity on ministry management in a local body of believers, while others focus on teaching. However, this does not negate the necessity of shepherding AND leading in tandem, especially for the man in vocational ministry designated as a Senior or Lead Pastor.

The second half of our study will be focused on the work of the spiritual shepherd both in the care of the individual sheep and the guidance of the local church as a whole. The emphasis will continue to be on *growing*. While some men may be more effective than others in one skill or another, one venue

---

[20]"The omission of the article from *teachers* seems to indicate that pastors and teachers are included under one class. The two belong together." Vincent, M. R. *Word Studies in the New Testament Volume 2*. McLean Virginia: Mac Donald Publishing CO, 1886, 858.

or another, in one stage of life or another, the fruitful pastor will not be focused on achieving a certain standard of ability or recognition, rather he is focused on consistent progress in the whole work of spiritual leadership.

Chapter 11

GROWING IN THE WORK OF A SHEPHERD

"Jane is dying in the hospital, and they want you to come." This brief message from one of our deacons at 4:00 AM both woke me up and gave me pause. Why did they want me, a 22-year-old, 4-months-out-of-Bible-college youth pastor to come to the hospital to be with a family I did not know whose middle-aged matriarch was about to die after a protracted battle with cancer? I was puzzled and scared. My pastor-father never discussed these kinds of calls. My senior pastor, who was on vacation, had not instructed me about such duties. I do not recall talking about such expectations in my pastoral education classes. Regardless of all that, I went to the hospital, and with her loved ones all around, watched her pass into glory. I prayed with the family and later met with them to plan a memorial service at which I spoke. Somehow, I stumbled through this assignment with some long-distance help from my senior pastor.

In the days since then, I have come to understand why the family (and the deacon) called for a spiritual leader (spoken very generously of my young self!); they did not know how to walk through this greatest of life's trials. God chose the nature of sheep to communicate the characteristics of those who yet needed to believe in Christ (Matthew 9:36) and those who had already believed (John 21:16) because sheep are notoriously sheepish! Left to themselves, they tend to wander aimlessly or follow the flock to their own harm. In the face of predators, they are virtually helpless. They only flourish under the care of a skilled caring shepherd.

God used the image of a shepherd to illustrate the role of a spiritual leader among His sheep. He was so intent on this imagery that He used it to refer to the church leadership role (Ephesians 4:11) and to the work that a man in that role should do among the flock God assigns to him (1Peter 5:1-4). There is no insult to be taken by God calling believers "sheep." Nor should any pride be assumed by the one called a "shepherd" of the flock. In God's wisdom, He created the Body of Christ to have leaders and followers, shepherds and sheep. In one sense, even those who are spiritual shepherds are sheep before Christ who is our ultimate shepherd.

The shepherd's direction: *Christlike perfection*

The literal shepherd was tasked with leading the sheep from place to place where they could find grass to eat, water to drink, and places to rest. Eventually, he would lead them back to the home of the owner to be sheared, some to be sold, some to be consumed, and a few to be used in the worship of God. All of this to benefit the owner of the sheep. The shepherd did not lead the sheep according to his own desires or theirs. He had a clear objective: the health, growth, and reproduction of the sheep to serve the owner.

God has given the spiritual shepherds of his flocks a similarly clear directive. The summary of that instruction is recorded in Ephesians 4:11-13, "He gave some…pastors and teachers, for the equipping of the saints for the work of service, to the building up of the body of Christ; until we all attain to the unity of the faith, and of the knowledge of the Son of God, to a mature man, **to the measure of the stature which belongs to the fullness of Christ**." God's goal for His sheep is *complete Christlikeness*. Paul expressed this as his personal mission in Colossians 1:28, "We proclaim Him [Jesus], admonishing every man and teaching every man with all wisdom, so that we may **present every man complete in Christ**."

The goal of a pastor's work is to be God's instrument to make and mature believers through a local church ministry.[21] Preaching the Word is not the goal, but a means to the goal. Changing the culture of a society is not the objective of church ministry, changing lives from sinful to God-honoring is. Church services should not exist just to inspire people, but to transform their lives. Children's church should go beyond childcare to planting the seeds of the gospel and training in Christlike behavior. Youth groups must go beyond fun and fellowship to make disciples of Christ. Every man who is called "pastor" must be leading the people God has entrusted to him toward a fuller, deeper life in Christ.

How can a pastor grow in directionality?

The old joke quotes an airline pilot who comes on the intercom telling the passengers, "I have bad news, our compass is broken, and we do not know where we are going. But there is good news too, we are making excellent time!" The fruitful pastor cannot settle for his church to be making aimless good time. Carrying on a busy ministry full of activities which may or may not be moving people toward Christlikeness cannot be acceptable. The only way to move toward Christ's goal for the church (Ephesians 5:27) is to **be clear about the destination** and to know how your church *is* and *is not* moving in that direction. Thus, the fruitful pastor must be a **student of his church**. Instead of putting his head in the proverbial sand, he listens and observes the ministry and searches the Scripture for God's standard of evaluation. He talks to God about what he sees, and he begins to formulate strategies for progress.

In his daily personal time with God, the pastor who would sharpen the focus of his people toward the pursuit of

---

[21] I realize that some men live out their pastoral call in settings other than the local church. My primary target is the majority of pastors who do serve in the local church, and I am emphasizing that pastors do not do the ministry alone but as part of the church they lead.

Christlikeness will aim **his prayer time for them on their needed spiritual growth,** not just on their presence at services and events or on their physical needs. When he sees them in the church or the community, his first question will not be, "Where were you" or "Will you be there" but, "How are you doing?" The fruitful pastor must work to make his way of thinking and speaking godlier if he would help his people focus on their genuine needs. As he works through this process, he will get a sense of needed growth in his church. He and his ministry leaders will Biblically evaluate their ministry and pray about their concerns. As they talk, pray, and seek the Lord together, they will envision necessary changes which will be executed as a team.

In public, especially in the prime weekend service(s), the pastor who would lead his people to be like Christ **does not talk about how many people are present** or absent. When he does it belies either his personal concern, or the pressure he feels from others, to count success in the quantity of attenders.[22] While an unintended consequence, the pastor's regular mention of the fullness or lack thereof in the worship room teaches his people to do the same, thus inadvertently building on the common human perspective of evaluating success by popularity. Instead, the fruitful pastor values individuals, however many of them may be present. Is God's Word worth sharing with one person? Then rejoice that more than one worshipper is present! A man who is only excited or fulfilled in sharing with a "full house" needs to check his motives.

A wonderful way to re-direct people toward God's destination for ministry is to **make a big deal out of baptism.** I learned a methodology many years ago from a pastor whose church was extremely fruitful over many decades, and it brought

---

[22] I acknowledge the value of knowing how many people are in church, but quantity must not be the goal. I also understand that good stewardship of time should press us to do our best to gather God's people and the seekers, so we maximize our efforts.

great blessing to my churches.[23] The godly pastor must constantly seek ways to reinforce critical truths, and one of the most important is giving public testimony of salvation through baptism. The occasion of baptism is a perfect time to enunciate the gospel and great themes of the Christian life like faith, witness, commitment, heaven, hell, and more. Instead of tacking baptism onto a service, the fruitful church leans into it full on, rejoicing with those taking a stand for Christ.

If a pastor yearns above all for his people (and others who don't yet know the Savior) to know life in Christ and all the blessing that life brings, he will be ever mindful of that destination. He will **talk** about the wonderful impact of Christ in life. He will **lead** his people to meaningful worship, not to gain a crowd or pander to preferences, but to give glory to the Savior for all he has done. He will **encourage** his people to give generously as God gave to them, not out of fear of financial failure or some misguided notion of mandatory "tithing." The pastor who would be fruitful keeps his people and the program of the church focused on becoming like Christ and helping others to do the same.

The shepherd's map: *the Bible*

The route that leads to the destination of increasing Christlike character in the Body of Christ is also given by God in Ephesians 4:11-15, "He gave some...**pastors and teachers, for** the equipping of the saints for the work of service, to the building up of the body of Christ; until we all attain to the unity of the faith, and of the knowledge of the Son of God, to a mature man, to the measure of the stature which belongs to the fullness of Christ...but, **speaking the truth** in love, may grow up in all things into Him who is the head--Christ." God's spiritual shepherds are called "pastor-teacher" because they are to lead

---

[23] See appendix "A" of this book for a summary of this method.

their flocks toward spiritual maturity by the communication of God's truth.

Paul was even more explicit with the connection between God's truth and Christlike character in these verses,

> "To them God willed to make known what are the riches of the glory of this mystery among the Gentiles, which is Christ in you, the hope of glory. Him we preach, warning every man and **teaching every man** in all wisdom, **that we may present every man perfect in Christ Jesus**" (Colossians 1:27-28).

There are several words used to refer to the communication of God's truth in the New Testament. In Colossians 1:28, "preach" is based on the same word transliterated elsewhere as "angel" and means to "proclaim"[24] a message. In Colossians 1:23 and 60 other times in the New Testament, the word "preach" comes from a word meaning to be a "herald" with a message to share.[25]

Another aspect of communicating God's truth is the word translated 77 times as, "gospel."[26] In the verb form, this word occurs 55 times and is translated "preached," and in several other ways based in the literal meaning of "good news."[27] Besides these words focused on the proclamation of truth, we have the Greek word "*didasko*" translated as teacher, teaching (*process*) and teaching or doctrine[28] (*content*). Suffice it to say, God made it abundantly clear throughout the New Testament

---

[24]Brown, Colin. *The New International Dictionary of New Testatment Theology Volume 3.* Edited by Colin Brown. Grand Rapids, MI: Zondervan, 1978, 44.
[25]Ibid., 44.
[26]Smith, J.B. *Greek-English Concordance to the New Testament.* Scottdale, PA: Mennonite Publishing House, 1955, 156.
[27]Ibid., 156
[28]Brown, Colin. *The New International Dictionary of New Testatment Theology Volume 3.* Edited by Colin Brown. Grand Rapids, MI: Zondervan, 1978, 44.

that the communication of His truth is vitally important. The fruitful shepherd speaks God's Word to help God's people move toward God's destination of Christlike character. (*For ease of communication I will use the word "preaching" extensively as a summary term for all kinds of communication of God's truth.*)

Where and when are you preaching?

This might seem like a silly question, but I assure you it is quite important. Too many times we think of preaching as something primarily done when the church is gathered. We think of hours of preparation, written refinement and standing before God's people to deliver the product of our toil. Paul gave Timothy a much broader instruction when he said, "Be ready" to preach (2 Timothy 4:2 NKJV). "The verb means to be ready, be at hand, stand by. The preacher of God's Word should *always* be ready...God's Word is *always* profitable and is *always* in season. Since sinners are *always* in season also, God's servant must show a readiness to minister the Word, even outside of "office" hours"[29] [*emphasis added*]. This instruction is intensified with the phrase, "in season and out of season." The words literally mean in a "good time, or a bad time."[30] We commonly call people on the cell phone and say, "Is this a good time?" because we don't want to intrude when they might be otherwise engaged. Paul told Timothy to always speak God's truth, whether welcome or not.

What this tells the fruitful pastor is that God's Word is ALWAYS what is needed, and he must ALWAYS be ready to bring it to bear on every situation. The easiest box to tick here is speaking to the gathered church. A little more challenging time for some is bringing God's Word to bear in the counseling setting. Do we somehow believe that God's Word changes lives when proclaimed in a church service but not in the counseling

---

[29]Kent, Homer A. *The Pastoral Epistles.* Chicago: Moody Press, 1975. 293.
[30]Thayer, Joseph Henry. *Thayer's Greek English Lexicon of the New Testatment.* Grand Rapids, Michigan: Zondervan , 1974, 21, 259.

room? Leadership (elders, deacons, etc.) discussions, decisions, and plans should certainly be accomplished under the guidance of God's truth. Those who are preparing for marriage need to consider God's ways for their life together. Those who are grieving a departed loved one or those suffering significant illness need to hear a word of God's comfort.

Perhaps the most important category of "where" is *anywhere*. We could call this "casual conversation" but that does not mean it is unimportant. "Let your speech always be with grace, seasoned with salt, that you may know how you ought to answer each one" (Colossians 4:6). God's truth ought to be a normal part of a pastor's way of thinking about *everything* and thus should come out of his mouth in all kinds of settings.

What are you preaching?

The words "Christ" and "preach, preached, or preaching" occur together at least 25 times in the New Testament in statements like this from the Apostle Paul, "Him we **preach**, warning every man and teaching every man in all wisdom, that we may present every man perfect in **Christ** Jesus" (Colossians 1:28). I am not of the persuasion that asserts that one can (and must!) preach Christ from every verse in the Bible. I *am* persuaded that salvation in Christ and the resulting life of growing sanctification should be integral to the communication of God's truth in the Body of Christ. If we are not connecting the salvation which only comes through Christ, to the commands about thoughts, behaviors, relationships, or church ministry, then we are teaching moralism. God has given everything we need for life and godliness *through* the knowledge of Christ.

The fruitful pastor needs to be on guard against non-Biblical ideas which slither into the Christian world and try to take the place of genuine Bible doctrine. Paul warned the Colossian believers about this when he wrote, "Beware lest anyone cheat you through **philosophy** and empty **deceit**, according to the **tradition of men**, according to the **basic principles of the world**, and not according to Christ" (Colossians 2:8). The problem Paul is addressing is the mixing of extra-Biblical so-called "truth" with actual truth. The key defining phrase is, "according to the basic principles of the world," which Vincent understands as "material contrasted with spiritual."[31]

A great deal of non-Biblical life-informing ideas are couched in scientific (material world) research and called "psychology." Many believers use these ideas to augment and fill in supposed gaps in God's truth for life, yet they are of the physical world, not revealed by God. In his excellent book on expository preaching, Dr. John MacArthur quotes Dr. John White, a Christian and Psychiatrist,

> "Until about fifteen years ago [quote is from the 1980's] psychology was seen by most Christians as hostile to the gospel. Let someone who professes the name of Jesus baptize secular psychology and present it as something compatible with Scripture truth, and most Christians are happy to swallow theological hemlock in the form of 'psychological insights.'"[32]

Imagine what Dr. White would say if he perused the "Christian Life" section in a Christian bookstore today!

Pastors need to always read books and listen to teaching with the filter of Biblical theology firmly in place. The Apostle Paul warned the Ephesian elders that the greatest dangers to their flock would come from within the church, "For I know this, that after my departure savage wolves will come in among you, not sparing the flock. Also, from ***among yourselves*** men will rise up, speaking ***perverse things***, to draw away the disciples after

---

[31]Vincent, M. R. *Word Studies in the New Testament Volume 3*. McLean, Virginia: MacDonald Publishing, 1886, 906.
[32]MacArthur, John. *Rediscovering Expository Preaching*. Dallas: Word Publishing, 1992, xvi.

themselves" (Acts 20:29-30). I cannot judge the motives of those who mix psychology and the Bible, but I can judge the product of their work and reject it (Matthew 7:20). When God's Word does not seem to have the answers for life, the problem is not with the Bible but with the expositor. Grabbing a resource that seems to readily answer a current problem, but has no Scriptural basis, is in effect to elevate such philosophy to the level of God's Word.[33] *Only God's Word applied in the power of the Spirit produces Christlike character.* The fruitful pastor studies God's Word for himself and gives ear to genuinely godly men who have studied the Word deeply, and in this process he finds God's answers for God's children.

There is a similar challenge with wisdom for leadership in the church. Via the old saw, "All truth is God's truth," it is not uncommon for spiritual leaders to seek insights for managing the local church from secular leadership experts. One such authority said this of his mentor, the noted business consultant, Peter Drucker, "Through Peter's writing, I had begun to understand the principles that were fundamental to understanding human interaction—not just the headline stuff, but the *assumptions that were at the heart of things across centuries.* They became my touchstones" [*emphasis added*].[34] Please know that I am not condemning Bob Buford as a man nor am I condemning everything he has taught, because I do not know him. What I know is that he believes he has learned truth about humanity from Peter Drucker who is quoted as saying, "I am not a born-again Christian. I went to church and tithed, but no, I am not a Christian."[35] Interestingly, the mission of the publisher

---

[33] I had a discussion with a missionary, who was sent out by a Biblically conservative church and mission agency, which came down to this statement question, "So you believe that God revealed truth through Sigmund Freud?" He answered, "Yes."
[34] Buford, Bob. *Drucker & Me.* Brentwood: Worthy Publishing, 2014, 27.
[35] Silva, Ken. *Was Peter Drucker a Christian.* June 11, 2012. https://www.apprising.org/2012/06/11/was-peter-drucker-a-christian-the-spin-versus-the-truth/.

of Buford's book, Worthy Publishing, is stated in the flyleaf as, "Helping people experience the heart of God."[36] Might there be some helpful ideas in Buford's book? Probably. However, the pastor who would lead and manage ("oversee") his church according to God's truth must start and complete his thinking and communicating from God's Word, and when he reads other ideas, he must carefully analyze them according to the ONLY source of truth, the Bible.

Fruitful preaching MUST be Biblical, and it also should be timely. I believe in the systematic teaching of God's Word, often lumped together with the term "expository preaching;" however, some men who begin a book of the Bible believe that there is nothing more important than to go passage by passage, week by week, without regard for anything happening in the world or the congregation. The fruitful pastor does not just pick a book of the Bible to preach through; he chooses Bible content which will address issues in his church and themes of seasons. He could start the Book of Matthew on the first Sunday of December thereby having a Christmas emphasis. He could work through Matthew but jump ahead in March/April to the passion week sections, then come back to the other chapters. Like Paul, we must, "declare the whole counsel of God" (Acts 20:27), but that does not mean we *must* do it in only one way. Preaching should be designed to move the flock toward the God-ordained destination of Christlike character. There are many good books on preaching and planning a preaching calendar.[37] As with all areas of ministry, the fruitful pastor will not assume he knows everything he needs about this aspect of shepherding but will seek input from other good men.

---

[36]Buford, Bob. *Drucker & Me.* Brentwood: Worthy Publishing, 2014, quoted from the bibliographic page, no page number listed.
[37]A few titles that have been helpful for me, "Biblical Preaching" by Haddon Robinson, Invitation to Biblical Preaching" by Donal Sunukjian, Communicating for a Change" Stanley & Jones, "12 Essential Skills for Great Preaching" Wayne McDill.

A vital way to learn what content is needed for the main service preaching calendar is to interact with the sheep away from the church. Visits to the home, workplace or hospital are ways to listen to and watch believers in their normal lives (not with the Sunday best clothes and smiles!). While you might not enjoy social media, following your people might be a way to learn about what they really think. Counseling sessions reveal themes of truth from God's Word not understood or appropriated. While we should never share personal information from these, we can glean topics that need emphasis, especially as we see themes repeated among various people. While I seldom *enjoy* watching the news, I do learn about the world around me as I do from reading the local newspaper. If we would communicate God's Word to those who are coming out of a worldly way of thinking, we should be consistently learning about their world.

How are you preaching?

By this question I mean to challenge your attitude in communication. Over 20 years ago I went to visit one of my daughters who was away at college. We went to her church which was Biblically strong but had some differences from my faith tradition. I entered the service with a critical eye, but I left with an epiphany about my own preaching. The Pastor's message had content very similar to what I would have said on the text, but there was one big difference, he was smiling! As I reflected on his manner, I realized that I tended to be a bit of a scolding parent in my preaching style emphasizing words like these, "Preach the word...CONVINCE, REBUKE, EXHORT," and almost ignoring the end of that verse, "with all **longsuffering** and **teaching**" (2 Timothy 4:2). Paul said that there should be several targets in how God's people minister to one another and this surely applies to the communication of God's Word, "**warn** those who are unruly, **comfort** the fainthearted, **uphold** the weak, be **patient** with all" (1 Thessalonians 5:14).

As I meditated on the Word and continued to reflect on what I experienced, I realized that I could just as easily call people up to the wonderful opportunity of Christlike living as I could thunder about the danger and guilt of sin. I resonate with a statement I read recently in an interview with noted Christian activist lawyer Michael Farris. He was asked, "If you could go back and give advice to your 30-year-old self, what would it be?" The 72-year-old founder of the Home School Legal Defense Fund replied, "**Learn to sing the song sweetly**. My lyrics were OK—even solid. But my melody needed work. The message I have been called to deliver is best delivered with both solid lyrics and a *sweet melody*" [*emphasis added*].[38] Yes, we must speak of turning from sin, but we also ought to speak of the blessed opportunity God has given us to live the Christ life.

The question of "how" you are preaching also extends to your **general style**. Do you stand behind a pulpit and read a manuscript or pace back and forth across all the real estate of the platform? Are you lively or mellow? Do you use technology (visual) to reinforce your message? Do you dress up or down or somewhere in-between? Do you hand out notes and how are they formatted? It is not my goal or gift from God to tell you exactly how to communicate God's truth, but I do have a challenge for your consideration; *does your style of delivery accomplish what you hope it will, given the text you are preaching and occasion of your message?* Above all, is your way of proclaiming God's truth enabling people to progress along the road to the destination of Christlike character?

Last Christmas I was at my home church[39] and the associate pastor who spoke on the incarnation was excited and

---

[38] Vincent, Lynn. "A Chat with Michael Farris." *World*, November 18, 2023: 72

[39] I have two home churches; this one is the one that I used to pastor, and they sent me out to my current role. The other home church is where I am a member and attend when not speaking elsewhere.

joyful. Clearly, the truth had touched his heart, and he was happily expounding on the doctrine of the eternal second person of the trinity taking on flesh so He could be our Savior. His enthusiastic animated communication of the truth drew me in and caused me to be excited and joyful and moved to worship. Good theology evokes wonder and worship and when expressed in a genuinely lively way infects the hearers with that same enthusiasm.

HOW can a pastor grow in the communication of God's Word?

The fruitful pastor who would communicate God's Word well must **be in the Word consistently** for his own spiritual growth. I have already spoken about this at length in chapter 4 as part of the process of growth, but here I would emphasize that one of the impacts of personal growth is a greater understanding of God's Word both as truth *known and* applied. If a man is not grappling with God's truth personally, he will not know the Word well nor will he know how to teach it to others.

The fruitful pastor should **memorize Scripture**, especially those significant verses and passages which he will need at his fingertips often in his work with the flock. Memorization is one way to do what the Old Testament called "meditating" on God's truth. "Meditate" is an onomatopoetic term, that is, it is an attempt to put a sound down in a written form.[40] This word is derived from the sound of someone mumbling or talking under their breath. In the Old Testament era the way people learned the Word of God was to hear it read by a priest, then to repeat it over and over as they walked home till it was memorized. This was the only way to have God's truth readily available in that time. Jason Nightingale, who is now with

---

[40]Vine, W. E. *Vine's Expository Dictionary of Biblical Words.* Nashville, TN: Thomas Nelson, 1985, 150.

the Lord, was a man who memorized whole books of the Bible and had a ministry sharing them in churches. He asserted that the key to memorization was repeated reading of the Scripture aloud, similar to the practice of meditating in the Old Testament era.

Whether memorizing or not, one of the keys to understanding the Scripture is repeated reading. Memorization is not the only way to accomplish this, but it is an excellent way. God has made it possible for us to understand His word through His Spirit, "Now we have received, not the spirit of the world, but the Spirit who is from God, that we might know the things that have been freely given to us by God. These things we also speak, not in words which man's wisdom teaches but which the Holy Spirit teaches, comparing spiritual things with spiritual" (1 Corinthians 2:12-13). However, God does not work in us without our effort. As we "hear" God's Word through multiple repetitions of it, the Holy Spirit enables us to deepen our understanding of it.

God also empowers **our study of the Word.** There are many excellent books on Bible study and preaching, so I will not attempt to write one here. I will advocate for a few practices that I think are crucial. The first two are mentioned above. Your personal time letting God apply His Word to you and your meditation on the Word through repeated reading and/or memorization will produce a rich yield over the years of teaching God's truth to others. In the formal time of studying, come to the Word with an open mind and let the Scripture dictate the sermon. Every pastor wants to call himself an "expositor," but even when we embrace a through-the-Bible book method of preaching, we can come to the Scriptures with our mind already set on certain ideas in a text. Instead, we need to read, study, pray, and let God bubble up the truth He wants emphasized in a certain time and place. The faithful preacher needs to study the Word and read the resources prayerfully over days and let God develop an understanding of His Word with an application for that time and place, and how to communicate it.

The fruitful pastor **builds his library** by obtaining books (paper or digital) that help with the part of God's Word he will be teaching. He listens to good preachers and tries to discern why they are effective, not to mimic them, but to glean principles that might be applied in his own way to his opportunities. Above all, he GROWS in his ability to communicate God's Word. He does not settle for just getting by. He does not assume that his knowledge or style of communication is without the need for improvement. He strives to be the best teacher God can make of him.

The fruitful pastor who would be an excellent public communicator of God's Word ought to learn from other effective communicators. That can be done in formal classes that he might take as part of an ongoing long-term educational program or could come in a seminar setting like the Simeon's Trust[41] which not only offers live classes, but also has recordings of their seminars. Beyond such formal education, the effective preacher will listen carefully to those he sits under and learn from their effectiveness. He can also learn by listening to recordings of good expositors not just for the content, but for the method of their communication.

The communication of God's Word is an activity that benefits greatly from giving a **listening ear** (see chapter 8) for feedback. In the counseling setting, people will push back and even argue against the truth you share. This dynamic kind of feedback can help the fruitful pastor refine the way he expresses truth. No one hears more sermons from a pastor than his wife. Her questions and critiques (hopefully given kindly and not right after church!) may be very helpful. Church members will have questions, challenges, and compliments. The growing pastor prayerfully considers all such input, believing it may be God

---

[41]https://simeontrust.org/

guiding Him through the Body of Christ (1 Corinthians 12). The man who is serious about developing as a pastor will seek out a brother he believes to be a highly effective preacher and ask for mentoring in this vital aspect of ministry.

Over the years I have made several changes in how I present God's truth on Sunday mornings. Early in my first lead pastor role, I realized that I needed to switch Bible versions to be more easily understood by the congregation. Years later, my wife gave me a nudge that turned into a major shift in my manner of preaching. I had occasionally used presentation software with my sermons, but she urged me to do it consistently. She noted that after giving a main point, as I would speak about it, if people's attention would wander, a look at the screen would bring them back on point. As I considered her input, I realized that including this visual tool would allow me to do several things better, so I made the change. These and other shifts in my approach to communication over the years have been propelled by the desire to share God's truth in a way that can be grasped by His people, not by how well I have adhered to a method of teaching.

We all learned a method of presenting God's Word though what is commonly called a "sermon" in Bible college or seminary or directly from a mentor. I'm not suggesting you throw it out, or radically change it, just that you regularly step back and evaluating to see if it is still as effective as it once was.

The shepherd's commitment: *personal ministry*

Given that the Shepherd is to lead the sheep toward spiritual growth, does this mean that the shepherd must always provide ministry on an individual level for every church member? That would be impossible in scope and implementation for a local church of an average size, much less those which are larger. In the days when the Bible was written the shepherd of four-footed sheep did not work alone, and neither should a pastor in a local church. (We will address the pastor's role of training church members to minister to one another more fully in the next section, but at this point we focus on those times when he should minister to individuals.) In the ancient times, the shepherd would call the sheep, and they would follow him to the pasture or the still water. When it was time to rest, they would be made to lie down together. In the same manner today's spiritual shepherd invests much of his time in leading the whole flock, through preaching and the broad church ministry. It is likely that he may also work with groups of various sizes such as a men's fellowship, a Sunday School class, or a home group.

But, like a shepherd in ancient Israel, when *one* sheep is injured, he does not throw the healing oil on the whole flock, rather he carefully applies it to the injured one. When one member wanders off in rebellion or foolishness the shepherd does not preach a message of correction to the whole flock, rather he goes after the singular sinner and helps that *one* to come back to the fold. There will be times when church members struggle with issues which some would say need "counseling," like anxiety, depression, relationship struggles and the like. While the word "counseling" scares some pastors off, it should simply be seen as individual discipleship to those sheep who are sinning, wandering, wondering, broken-hearted, or in some way not experiencing the joy and peace of Christ.

Of course, not every child of God needs the same amount of personal pastoral care. Generally, those who may need the most individual help will be new believers, those who have failed to mature in Christ, and mature Christians who have fallen into a new trial. For example, it is not uncommon to find a mature believer married to one who has refused to grow or who has come to a place of disobedience, and that couple will reach out for help in their crisis. Another ubiquitous life event most believers need help with is death (all in this situation need *some* help, but some need *much* help). This trial touches all human beings and for some it will be particularly difficult. Along with

Charles Jefferson, I believe every pastor should readily work individually with those sheep who need it,

> It is the mission of the pastor to minister to minds diseased; to pluck from the memory a rooted sorrow; to raze out the written troubles of the brain; and with some sweet oblivious antidotes, to cleanse the stuffed bosom of the perilous stuff, which weighs upon the heart. There is always someone ailing in the parish, not physically only, but mentally, morally, spiritually. The diseases of the soul are numerous, and the remedies provided by the almighty are efficacious only when applied by a skilled practitioner.[42]

The entire tone of Psalm 23 speaks of a very personal kind of ministry done by the Divine Shepherd who is the model for the contemporary undershepherd. The fruitful pastor must *learn* to do personal ministry. Very few Bible College or Seminary graduates come into a church leadership role confidently prepared to help individual sheep through their unique challenges. To reject doing personal ministry because it is not comfortable, or to excuse it because it is not thought to be one's gift, is to deny the meaning of the primary designation of the spiritual leader which is pastor—shepherd. The ancient shepherd did not stand on a hill and shout instructions to his sheep. He walked with them calling them onto the right path and guiding them along the journey.

One of the great promises of God for the believer is also true for pastors, "No temptation (test) has overtaken you except such as is common to man; but God is faithful, who will not allow you to be tempted beyond what you are able, but with the temptation will also make the way of escape, that you may be able to bear it" (1 Corinthians 10:13). God allows challenging,

---

[42] Jefferson, Charles. *The Minister as Shepherd.* Manila: Living Books for All, 1973, 51.

unwelcome, and hard circumstances to foment spiritual growth in believers. How should pastors know if they can "handle" a given need for ministry? The simple answer is this, if he is in it, he can handle it—in Christ through the power of the Spirit. Every situation the pastor finds himself in has been allowed by God for His good and His glory and to grow up the believer and the pastor. I suspect that many pastors shun personal ministry because the problems people ask for help with seem too big for them to handle. This is compounded by the common societal truism that some difficulties like depression, anxiety, grief, homosexuality, etc. are best left to professionals. Between the fear of the issues and assumed lack of professional skill, men come to believe they are ill-equipped to help.[43]

    When God causes members of the church to call for help, the fruitful pastor accepts the assignment believing that God has given it to him and will empower him to help his people.[44] Without minimizing anyone's pain, after many years of personal ministry my observation would be that there are various levels of intensity and complexity to the problems God's people experience. If a pastor is untested in some aspect of personal ministry (as I was with the death call I spoke about at the beginning of this section) he needs to believe that God will only call him to situations he can handle with His help. When a pastor feels ill-equipped, he should get on his knees in prayer and open the Word to find answers and go forth to do his best. It may be rough; he may have to back-track or even apologize for a mistake here or there, but he also might find himself to be

---

[43] I have counseled many people referred from churches whose pastors do not counsel even though they believe in a Biblical approach.

[44] This is not at all to ignore the need for teamwork in the church. If a pastor does not feel prepared for when certain needs appear, by all means he should find a brother or sister who can be part of a care team. But he does not send the church member down the street to some supposedly professional helper who has all the answers which the pastor does not. Above all, he GROWS in this aspect of personal ministry.

effectively used of God to liberate someone from the tyranny of their sinful condition, or to help them walk through what seems like an overwhelming hardship. This is exactly what God calls all believers to when He says, "Brethren, if a man is overtaken in any trespass, you who are spiritual restore such a one in a spirit of gentleness, considering yourself lest you also be tempted. Bear one another's burdens, and so fulfill the law of Christ" (Galatians 6:1-2).

The shepherd's Mission: Growing in Evangelism

One of the specific commands the Apostle Paul put in Timothy's job description was this, "Do the work of an evangelist" (2 Timothy 4:5). This helps us understand that the reference to "evangelist" (Ephesians 4:11) was about a unique spiritual gift. I agree with MacArthur who says, "New Testament evangelists were missionaries and church planters (much like the apostles, but without the title and miraculous gifts)."[45] Even though there is little evidence to categorically identify this gift, we do have the example of Philip in Acts 8. My point is simply that whether a local church pastor has the gift of evangelism (and there seems to be such a thing) he is to be engaged in the work of sharing God's good news with unbelievers.

How does the fruitful shepherd grow in the work of evangelism? He must be a firm believer himself with a full understanding of the gospel. The man with doubts about his salvation MUST find the answers and be settled in Christ BEFORE taking on the role of leading believers in their own fruitful living. With a clear understanding of his own salvation, he should be ready to lead others to Christ; however, this too is an area of growth.

In Bible college I learned the "Romans Road" using passages from the book of Romans to help others understand salvation and how to become a child of God. In my first

---

[45]MacArthur, John. *Ephesians*. Chicago: Moody, 1986, 143.

pastorate the whole church was encouraged to take an "Evangelism Explosion" class. This was not a suggestion for me as my senior pastor mandated my participation. At times I still use some of the ideas and illustrations from that program when I am sharing with unbelievers. A few years later I heard the creationist teacher Ken Ham who asserted that evangelism in this post-modern world needs to start at Genesis 1:1. He had many helpful ideas which were also added to my preaching of the gospel and practice of evangelism.

The fruitful pastor should consider how each Bible message connects to the truth of salvation. After preaching on any area of sin and righteousness, he should remind the congregation of the power necessary to obey the truth which only comes from the Holy Spirit who takes up residence when a person believes in Christ. Without this gospel emphasis, an unbeliever could leave the church service thinking he must do the works of God on his own, or he may be so discouraged at not being able to obey God that he will give up on Christianity. Connecting the gospel to the Christian life shows both believers and unbelievers how God intends for us to live like Jesus. Personally, I appreciate those converts who say they were saved sitting in the pew in church. No one was personally pressing them, but the Holy Spirit did the convicting through the Word of God.

The fruitful pastor also engages unbelievers in gospel conversation. Whether with a retiree at McDonalds, a teen who has been attending youth group, or a broken soul who has come for counseling, he is ready and eager to share God's truth when the opportunities present themselves.

The shepherd's mandate: *growing a church of ministers*

We come back to our key instruction from God about the work of the pastor and the flock under his care. Please note the bold type in this text about the local church.

And He Himself gave...some pastors and teachers, for the **equipping of the saints** for the **work of ministry**, for the **edifying of the body of Christ**, till we **all** come to the unity of the faith and of the knowledge of the Son of God, to a perfect man, to the measure of the stature of the fullness of Christ; that we should no longer be children, tossed to and fro and carried about with every wind of doctrine, by the trickery of men, in the cunning craftiness of deceitful plotting, but, speaking the truth in love, may grow up in all things into Him who is the head--Christ--from whom the **whole** body, joined and knit together by what **every joint** supplies, according to the effective working by which **every part** does its share, causes growth of the body for the **edifying of itself** in love. Ephesians 4:11-16

If we summarized this into a process it would look something like this: Christ gave pastor-teachers to communicate His truth to the church members, so they; whole body, every joint, every part, will be able to edify (help each other grow up), resulting in the maturing of the Body of Christ. The fruitful pastor does not just try to help individual members of his church become like Christ, he helps them to mature so they can serve one another in the church and evangelize the world. It is very easy to fall into a comfortable routine in church services and ministries where we rely on the same few people for many things most of the time. Involving new people in ministry means we must train them and put up with some lack of ability along the way to proficiency. The fruitful pastor is consistently watching his flock to see who is ready to move into a new/different/more challenging role. He works to give away his own responsibilities to those he trains as much as possible.

For most of my ministry life, I was the preacher and the worship leader. As a young man I was not wise enough to be looking for a recruit I could train, I was just trying to stay above water (and I am certain my senior pastor expected me to do certain things myself!). Years later, the day came when a promising young man joined our worship team. I could readily see that he had the heart and talent (but not the skill) to lead our church in praise to God. Over a substantial period of a time, as he became comfortable playing with the team, I gradually brought him up to the front of the platform with me. Then I had him begin to plan the service while I coached him. Then the day came when he led, and I sat down and enjoyed worshipping! In my last church young people were welcomed into the ministry in many ways. One of those young men is now the youth pastor of that church.

In my ministry travels as a church network director, I regularly saw pastors doing much of the morning service. They read the Scripture, pray, give the announcements and sometimes are also on the worship team. Both they and their church would be better served by finding people and training and coaching them and turning them loose. Paul's charge to Timothy is still binding on pastors today, "And the things that you have heard from me among many witnesses, commit these to faithful men who will be able to teach others also" (2 Timothy 2:2). I realize that this is speaking directly about pastor-teachers, but the principle applies to all elements of ministry according to Ephesians 4:11-16. *The fruitful pastor is oriented toward growing leaders, not just collecting listeners.*

How does a pastor **"equip the saints for work of ministry?"** He must know the sheep and the ministry needs (and he should equip other leaders to do this also). He must encourage people to tackle new roles in which he, and others, gives them training. Often seeing someone in one area of service will give the pastor a vision for other work they could be doing. I found a wonderful couple to help in my youth ministry by looking at the AWANA club! I stole the best people I could find, and then others were able to fill in the gaps in AWANA as their own first ministry involvement.

Part of this equipping of the saints for ministry is **helping them be ready to share the gospel.** As mentioned above, there are many programs which can be useful to help Christians be fully ready to share the gospel in their circle. A fruitful pastor may not be the best evangelist in the church, so he finds that gifted individual and helps him teach others how to share the good news. He cannot retreat behind his gift of pastor-teacher with the mistaken notion that he is free of the responsibility of leading his church to do the work commanded by Christ.

In Acts 6 we read of a need in the "First Baptist Church of Jerusalem," namely, a better organized social welfare program. Instead of the apostles divvying up the work, in conjunction with the congregation, they found seven men and deployed them into a new ministry. This should be happening regularly in a fruitful church. When there is a new need, a ministry can be created and staffed by those with the appropriate gifts. The fruitful pastor collaborates with other leaders to identify needs and find the right church members to fill those needs.

Every church has turnover (both for good and bad reasons) which results in a constant need for people to take on new responsibilities so the ministry can continue and expand. As members of the local church become more mature in Christ, they are prepared to take on new and greater responsibilities. The fruitful pastor is aware of how his people are growing and seeks to guide their placement in appropriate ministries. As he does this over time, he becomes a shepherd of shepherds with a dynamic team of servants building up one another in the church.

Ideas/Questions for Application

Throughout this section there have been ideas and suggestions on how to grow in the various aspects of shepherding. Begin by reviewing those suggestions and consider your ministry in light of them. Below are some summary statements with more suggestions.

Directionality: How sharp is your focus on shepherding your people toward Christlikeness?

- Review the recording of the weekend church service to see how many times you mentioned the quantity of people present or who was absent.

- If you have a mission statement, review it to see if it is about leading people and the church to be like Christ. If you don't have a mission statement, write one in conjunction with your leadership group.

The map: To what degree is God's Word your guide toward the destination of Christlikeness?

- Review any curriculums you use with adults. Are they truly Bible based?

- Review your last 4 sermons. Do they have clear applications to help people think and act like Christ?

- Review your last leadership meeting. What part did God's truth have in your interaction?

Personal ministry: How well are you caring for the sheep in your flock individually?

- Do you counsel your people when they ask for help? If you shun this kind of ministry, evaluate why and create a plan to become confident in it.

- Do you visit your people in their homes, workplaces, hospitals, etc.? If you struggle with this, find a pastor brother who can mentor you in it.

Evangelism: How often is the gospel emphasized in all aspects of ministry?

- Review your last 4 sermons to see if you presented the gospel in a way that showed its connection to your key sermon idea.

- Review your church calendar to see what you are doing to connect with unbelievers. When was the last time you spoke about the Lord to an unbeliever? If you need help with this, find a brother that is good at it and learn from him.

Developing a church of ministers: Are you consistently working to develop every believer into a functional part of the church ministry?

- Can you identify several people who have recently taken on a new ministry in your church?

- Do you have a plan to bring people into a ministry and help them succeed?

- What duty of yours are you actively trying to teach others to do?

Chapter 12

GROWING IN THE WORK OF AN OVERSEER

As I asserted in the introduction to the section on shepherding, there are two aspects to the work of a pastor, and they often (always?) interplay. We do not need to divide things into absolute boxes in order to understand and apply the truth. We have been considering the shepherd's work of caring for the members of his flock which in our day is often called "pastoral" work. This has already overlapped with the other broad aspect of his work; leadership to which we now turn our attention fully.

"People do what you inspect, not what you expect." This pithy statement by the maintenance director at the college I attended was an early leadership lesson to me. It was a bit jarring when I heard it and I had to ponder it for quite some time before I began to grasp the truth of it. Interestingly, it falls in line with the Greek word for church leadership translated "bishop" in the KJV/NKJV and more literally translated by the NIV/NASB as "overseer." It comes from a word that means "to look or watch," and a preposition which means "over."[46] It is used in both the noun and verb forms and denotes "the activity of looking at or paying attention to a person or thing."[47] Before it was used in the Scripture to speak of spiritual leaders in the Body of Christ, it was a common term for governmental workers

---

[46]Vine, W. E. *Vine's Expository Dictionary of Biblical Words.* Nashville, TN: Thomas Nelson, 1985, 67.
[47]Brown, Colin. *The New International Dictionary of New Testament Theology.* Edited by Colin Brown. Vol. 1. Grand Rapids, MI: Zondervan, 1975, 188.

of various kinds.[48] God took a common term for leadership/management and brought into the church to help His people understand what a shepherd was to do.

As already mentioned, the work of a spiritual leader in a local church has two key elements: helping the sheep to grow spiritually (pastor) and guiding the ministry of the members of the church to one another and the unsaved world (overseer).[49] The New Testament has much to say about this aspect of the pastor's work, especially in the books commonly referred to as the "pastoral" epistles. In these books addressed to Timothy and Titus, we have the privilege of listening in as the Apostle Paul instructs two pastors in how to lead their respective local churches. There is an overlap of the content in these three books and there are some distinctive instructions. God chose to give us these truths in real life examples, which helps us more readily apply them in our situations.

The necessity of leadership

"I wrote to the church, but Diotrephes, who loves to have the preeminence among them, does not receive us" (3 John 1:9). It would appear that a man named Gaius (3 John 1:1) was one of the elders, if not the leading elder of this church. It could be that Diotrephes was also an elder, but whether he was or not, we know for certain that for selfish reasons he kept the Apostle John away from the church! Quite obviously, the Apostle John would always upstage any pastor then as he would today, even though he would be the last person to accentuate his

---

[48] Brown, Colin. *The New International Dictionary of New Testament Theology.* Edited by Colin Brown. Vol. 1. Grand Rapids, MI: Zondervan, 1975, 189.

[49] Because of the misuse of the term "bishop" by the Roman Catholic Church and others who would make it into a ranked office above the local church pastor, I will use the term "overseer" to refer to the leadership and management aspects of the work of a local church pastor.

position or experience. How great would it be to have the Apostle John as a guest speaker in church!

There are always men (and occasionally women) who want to be THE key leader of a local church. Some call it a self-designated "church boss." Not only are there those who would take leadership that does not belong to them, there are men in vocational ministry who think that their call is only to preach and that others should be leading. While I believe in a plurality of elders, when possible (either vocational or volunteer), the lead Pastor cannot abdicate his role because of the spiritual nature of leadership.[50] A local church deacon relayed to me how the previous pastor said, "You deacons are to lead the church, it's not my job." In reality that pastor just did not know how to work with a group of leaders and did not like anything that resembled confrontation.

Often, those who want to control the church have less than spiritual motives, like Diotrephes (2 John 1:9). He simply liked being the top man. Some who try to control the church are motivated by their singular ways of seeing the ministry. They may believe that the church should not spend money but save it up—to spend on their priorities. I knew of a man who was antagonistic to music ministry—until the church had a country gospel group for a concert. Whatever the reason, the single vocational pastor in most churches,[51] or the senior pastor in a multiple staff church, is the only person whom everyone agreed should be the key leader. Dear reader, please understand, I do

---

[50] I am not arguing against a team of elders who may create a system in which one man emphasizes administration and another preaching, and the others taking parts of the ministry. I am advocating for the necessity of leadership being an integral part of the role of shepherd.

[51] The current average church in America is 65 people making it highly likely that there is only one vocational pastor. Earls, Aaron. "Small Churches Continue to Grow in Number but Not in Size." lifewayresearch.com. October 20, 2021. https://research.lifeway.com/2021/10/20/small-churches-continue-growing-but-in-number-not-size/.

not subscribe to the "pastor as dictator" model. However, someone will lead the church, and God thinks it should be someone qualified as an elder and recognized as a shepherd/overseer. That is why Paul told Timothy to lead—and to teach, in that order in the book of 1 Timothy.

I called a pastor to ask what had happened that caused him to resign from what seemed to be a thriving small-church ministry. He told me that when he came to the church, he had not tried to lead the overall work because of some dominant laymen already in place. He told me that the past five years of ministry were good, but that in the turmoil of the Covid era, he resigned because of a problem created by the very people he allowed to lead without him. He believed he could do ministry and let the other leaders "run" (his word) the church, which worked fine, until it did not. Not only did he leave, but some of the people also left because of how he was treated. This brought the church into another round of struggle with a new pastor working with the same dominating men.

Sheep need a shepherd because God has empowered the spiritual leader(s) to know where the sheep need to go (Christlikeness), and how to lead them there (God's Word). Sheep need a shepherd, but not all of them want one. Sheep need a shepherd but sometimes the shepherd will have to use the rod and staff of God's Word to correct them and direct them to be productive for the Lord who owns them.

The basis of leadership

The most important **qualification for leadership is character and the source of godly character is salvation.** Paul opened his second letter to Timothy recounting his awareness of Timothy's salvation. Paul was "mindful of the sincere faith" (1:5) which was in him, and which was the basis of Paul's first instruction in v.6, "stir up the gift of God which is in you." I feel a bit like Paul in Philippians 3:1 when he acknowledged the repetition of what he was about to say by exhorting the listeners of how important the truth was. So here dear reader, again I ask you to look in your heart and be certain that you are a born-again believer in Christ as Savior. No amount of leadership reading or training or technique will enable you to lead a local church to genuine fruitful ministry if you are not in Christ. Without the power of Christ, you might assent to all the Biblical truths about the pastoral role, but you will not have the strength or wisdom to live them out. Without the indwelling Holy Spirit to enable your understanding and empower the living of God's truth, you will struggle to properly apply God's instructions, and you will ignore those things you find impossible.

The **second aspect of character** that empowers spiritual leadership is an **exemplary life.** I will not repeat what I have written in earlier chapters on the importance of the pastor's personal walk with Christ, but I will lean into the truth enunciated by Paul in 1 Timothy 4:12, "Let no one despise your youth, but be an **example** to the believers in word, in conduct, in love, in spirit, in faith, in purity." Paul enlarged on this instruction in 6:11, "...**pursue** righteousness, godliness, faith, love, patience, gentleness." Kent Hughes summarizes the truth wonderfully, "So we see that Paul is telling Timothy that Christian leadership is a matter of godly character from beginning to end. *The ministry is a character profession.* Godly character creates moral authority. Ultimately, godly character wins over those who would naturally look down on one's youth."[52]

There is nothing more galling than a person who stands to condemn sin, then lives in that sin themselves. There is nothing more disheartening than listening to a man set a high bar for what it means to act like Christ, then to find out he does not live what he preaches. Even worse is the pastor who is living in sin, so he soft-pedals teaching on his weakness, or maybe in compensation he leans in extra hard against the very sin he is

---

[52]Chapell, R. Kent Hughes & Bryan. *1 & 2 Timothy and Titus.* Wheaton: Good News Publishers, 2000, 115.

practicing. The pastor's personal character MUST match his proclamation of God's truth from the pulpit. His life MUST match his words, else why would anyone follow him?

Every pastor will be criticized, opposed, and vilified at some point(s) in their ministry. When that happens, they will be tempted to argue, retaliate, and demonize those who attack. There will be lengthy discussions of matters that seem simple. There will be other men on his leadership team who do not want to do what the Scripture plainly instructs. In these moments the fruitful pastor MUST run to the Lord and come back with a fresh reserve of strength to act like Christ.

I know of a pastor who served for many years in his church alongside some good men and a dominating deacon. An issue needing a decision came to a point where the deacon did not agree with the pastor. The chairman of the deacons went to the inflexible man and said, "If you make us chose between you and the pastor, we're choosing the pastor." This was no power play by the pastor because he did not force the choice. The deacons followed him willingly because of years of godly character-based leadership. A pastor who chooses to dominate can often "get things done." He may even build a large ministry, but eventually something breaks, and the ruinous aftermath often outweighs the good done during such a man's tenure. (*Oh, and the inflexible deacon left the church apparently because he could not control anymore!*)

The direction of leadership

It is vital as we begin to consider the pastor's work of leading the church to remember the goal of that leadership which has been summarized very well by John Piper, "Spiritual leadership is knowing where God wants people to be and taking the initiative to get them there by God's means in reliance on

God's power."[53] Where God wants His people to be is mature in Christ (Ephesians 4:13). The pastoral leader must keep this destination crystal clear in his thinking because a host of competing goals will present themselves.

One of the most dangerous and consistent substitutes for spiritual fruitfulness is increasing size.[54] The enemy of our souls is driven by pride (Isaiah 14), and he has built our society to entice our fleshly desires (Ephesians 2:1-3), which includes pride and its brothers (Galatians 5:19-21). The resulting condition of the world around us appeals to our humanity, and we are tempted to live like unbelievers chasing those things which feed our pride (1 John 2:15-16) and cause us to think the church is doing well if there is an increase of "nickels and noses." The cure for this deadly syndrome is to stay focused on the spiritual growth of believers and outreach to unbelievers with a sincere full gospel presentation. The way we do those two things is to search God's Word for **HIS** objectives for ministry. Obedience to those objectives will ensure that we are trying to arrive at His desired destination for the church. As Paul said, we plant and water the gospel seed and leave the increase up to God (1 Corinthians 3:6-7).

With the mandate of making mature disciples of Christ (those who "observe all things," Christ taught) as the destination of true fruitful ministry, the leaders of a church must **envision what is needed to enable progress** toward that goal. This is essentially what the Apostle Paul did for Timothy and Titus when he sent the instructions for their ministries. "Here is what you need to do…1,2,3." Paul knew the churches and gave a "to-do" list that would both correct problems and empower development. This is what the spiritual leaders of a church must do consistently, especially at the beginning of a new year or

---

[53]Piper, John. *Brothers, We are Not Professionals.* Nashville: Broadman & Holman, 2002, 11.
[54]Please know that I am not against growth. In fact, I believe that if the church is doing fruitful ministry, there will be growth.

designated new ministry year. An honest review of what has gone well and what needs improvement must be done along with addressing new needs or problems that arise as the congregation ebbs and flows.

The objectives of leadership
Doctrinal purity

One of the most important roles of leadership in a church is doctrinal purity. Paul makes this priority #1 in his letter to Timothy on how to be a pastor, "As I urged you when I went into Macedonia--remain in Ephesus that you may charge some that they teach no other doctrine" (1 Timothy 1:3). The theme of doctrinal purity is also mentioned directly in many passages like 1 Timothy 6:3, Galatians 1, Ephesians 4:14, Colossians 2, Titus 1:9-11, and the book of 2 John. Doctrinal purity is based in the belief that a Bible text has one meaning, not many. To assert that it can have many meanings is to assert that there is no definitive meaning, thereby rendering the commands to doctrinal purity meaningless. Contrary to popular desire, God's Word is definitive on the issues, and able to be understood. The fruitful pastor must rightly understand the Scripture and lead the entire church to the same.

Equally important with a commitment to right doctrine is the reason for that commitment, stated succinctly in 1 Timothy 1:5, "The purpose of the commandment is love from a pure heart, from a good conscience, and from sincere faith." Only true doctrine from God himself can bring a person to saving faith in Christ and help them grow into a fully mature disciple. It is not loving to water down, dumb down, or relativize God's truth. No one is helped by a partial gospel or a contemporized notion of sin and righteousness. God does not grade on a curve, nor does He negotiate with those who do not like His standards. We must speak in love but what we must speak is the truth (Ephesians 4:15).

How does the pastoral leader maintain right doctrine?

The most vital starting point is the pastor's perception of truth and error. A shepherd who is intent on leading his people in genuine doctrine must grow in his understanding of right doctrine so he can perceive wrong doctrine before it infects his flock. A literal shepherd knows the plants that are poisonous and the water that is polluted so he can lead his flock away from them. Presuming that a pastor has a proficiency in Scripture knowledge before he becomes the leader of a flock, he must grow to have an ever-deepening grasp of God's truth through a personal in-depth study of scripture. He must read not only reference material and commentaries to help with his interpretation of the passages he is teaching, but also systematic theology to insure his awareness of many broad issues. Because the church world is ever evolving, the careful shepherd should read journals, periodicals, and news in paper or online. As I write this, some of the current theological debates are, can women be pastors? Is homosexuality sinful? Is the Old Testament needed? And all of the classic arguments against Scripture advanced by the haters. Books and articles are regularly written about these issues both for and against. While the pastor cannot read everything, he should grow in his ability to give excellent answers to difficult issues when questions are asked.

One of the skills that grows with years of pastoral experience is doctrinal discernment, the ability to see falsehood starting to develop before it is full-blown heresy. When a well-known evangelical preacher makes statements in a sermon saying that the Old Testament is not needful,[55] a mental red flag should go up in the careful shepherd's mind. While he does not run to the pulpit to castigate such a man, he should keep an eye and ear on him and take great care reading or listening to

---

[55]Mohler, Albert. "Albert Mohler." *albertmohler.com.* August 10, 2018, https://albertmohler.com/2018/08/10/getting-unhitched-old-testament-andy-stanley-aims-heresy.

anything from him. The fruitful shepherd is not caught flat-footed when such a man later speaks out full-blown heresy. This doesn't mean that the faithful shepherd is constantly critical, rather he is consistently careful with any input he receives, or ideas passed to him or that he might pass on to his flock.

With a clear understanding of right doctrine, the fruitful pastor ensures that his church has a Biblical **doctrinal statement** which is communicated to all, especially those who become formal members of the church. While formal membership is not commanded in the Bible, it is the most useful way to live out the instructions of the Bible (application) about church life in our North American society. There are several current books with a full discussion of church membership so I will not try to replicate them here. Suffice it to say, the well-organized church has a membership process, and it is a prime beginning point for creating and maintaining doctrinal purity. Everyone coming into the church knows what the church believes. This enables the leadership to expect the members to hold to those teachings. A vital part of passing on right doctrine is using sound curriculum for all Bible study classes. For teachers who write their own curriculum, there must be some kind of observation or inspection process to make sure the pure truth is being taught.

The second, and (should be) obvious, way a pastor maintains right doctrine in the church is by **doctrinally sound teaching.** I do not mean that his teaching/preaching should sound like a systematic theology textbook, rather that he thoroughly considers both the meaning of each individual text (via grammar, history, authorial intent, etc.) AND how that passage fits into the whole of Scripture. Some things sound good and seem like they will preach easily, that is, make an eloquent message, yet they are not actually present in a particular passage. This might be the most common error men make, preaching something Biblically true but not from the text at hand. Do the work, wrestle with the text, and preach truth...always!

The pastor who would maintain right doctrine must also **teach his people how to interpret the Bible** WHILE he teaches them the truth. The literal method of interpreting the Bible has rules or guidelines that steer the interpreter. When a pastor shares God's Word, he should succinctly state why the meaning is what it is without turning the sermon into a Bible college lecture. The Sunday School hour or some planned smaller group sessions ARE the place to teach systematic theology, hermeneutics, and the like, directly. In my last church I spent two years teaching an adult Sunday School class working through a curriculum entitled, "Through Bible Doctrine in a Year." I took more than a year to lead my people in thinking through God's truth. Later as we were preparing to send out a short-term missionary, we realized that she needed some theological training, so I organized a week-night class. A few people came and studied with the missionary as we worked through a one-volume doctrine textbook.

Last, but not least, the fruitful pastor **corrects those who stray** doctrinally. A pastor does not have the luxury of pretending nothing is wrong and hoping the error will miraculously disappear. Paul gives us a very powerful example of this in Galatians 2:11, "Now when Peter had come to Antioch, I withstood him to his face, because he was to be blamed." Wow, I would have liked to be a fly on that wall! Paul confronted Peter and he changed, and future Christianity was protected. The word "heresy" is a transliteration of a Greek word which has a root meaning of "to choose."[56] It was used to refer to those who had made a choice to join with others who had made the same choice[57] which is why in Titus 3:10 it is translated as "divisive" (KJV, NKJV, NIV) or "factious" (NASB); "Reject a divisive man after the first and second admonition."

---

[56]Thayer, Joseph Henry. *Thayer's Greek English Lexicon of the New Testament.* Grand Rapids, Michigan: Zondervan, 1974, 16.
[57]Brown, Colin. *The New International Dictionary of New Testament Theology.* Edited by Colin Brown. Vol. 1. Grand Rapids, MI: Zondervan, 1975, 533.

The fruitful and faithful pastor confronts wrong doctrine because those who hold it will not stop until they have influenced the whole church or some part of it to join their group.

Moral purity

The common morality of the world is the result of the agenda of the Evil One (Ephesians 2:1-3) which results in humanity living, "**In the lusts** of our flesh, **fulfilling the desires of the flesh** and of the mind" (v. 3). Those desires include adultery, fornication, uncleanness, lewdness" (Galatians 5:19). I fully realize that I did not need to write those last two sentences because everything we see and hear through media and common life around us is drenched in a sexual emphasis. In my lifetime, homosexual activity has gone from illegal to in-vogue. No longer does someone who identifies as gay or lesbian need to hide, now they are celebrated and allowed to be married to one another. Pornography, which was illegal, gradually crept onto shelves behind the counter in stores, and is now widely available via every smartphone, tablet, computer, or cable-attached television. The barrage of sexualized content has changed social values so that those who practice Biblical morality are in the smallest minority. I realize that I am not telling you anything new, but I am stressing this here because it must be addressed by the shepherd(s) of local churches.

Churches develop an internal culture as values are taught and experienced over time. God's standard (value) regarding sexuality is clear, "Marriage is honorable among all, and the bed undefiled; but fornicators and adulterers God will judge" (Hebrews 13:4), yet it gets muddied by the constant drone of sin in our world. The Apostle wrote some words to the Corinthian church that are still shocking today. They had a man in their congregation who was either in an incestuous relationship with his mother, or committing adultery with his stepmother, and the church's response was the most scandalous part, "You are puffed up, and have not rather mourned" (1 Corinthians 5:2). This church, full of newer believers, was living as they always had. The individual sin was bad enough, but the impact on the group was worse. In v. 6 of the same chapter, we read Paul's exhortation, "Do you not know that a little leaven leavens the whole lump?" In other words, moral sin left unchecked breeds a culture of acceptance or at least ignoring sin in the church.

How does the fruitful pastor create a culture of sexual righteousness?

First and foremost, he lives in moral purity as I mentioned in chapter 9. He must consistently fight and win the battle with his own flesh so he can know how to teach others to do the same. His heart must break for those who hurt themselves and others with sexual sin.

He must **preach and teach** the Word of God clearly and forthrightly on this vital topic. After seeing some particularly heinous results of sexual immorality in my work as a police chaplain, I decided to preach through 1 Thessalonians, in part so I would come to the section on sexual purity in chapter 4. A few years ago, after homosexual marriage became legal in our state,[58] I preached a series of two messages about homosexuality in which I worked hard to ensure that I was "speaking the truth IN love" but I did not hesitate to speak the truth. When asked to speak to a Christian school chapel once, I gave a message entitled, "It's OK to disobey" in which I did my best to lovingly teach the children that they should not obey adults if asked to do sexual activities. As a youth pastor, on several occasions I shared God's truth about right and wrong sexuality in as much detail as I thought prudent with my high school-age teens. When I did this, I had 100% attention. They wanted to know the truth, perhaps because the people in their lives were not talking about

---

[58] I live in Washinton State which was one of the first to legalize homosexual marriage.

sex, leaving them to get their information from the society around them.

Preaching about sexual behavior must go beyond what is wrong and clearly emphasize what is right. It must communicate the ramifications of sinful and righteous behavior. When we share God's "whys" alongside God's "dos and don'ts" we give people regulation with motivation. Certainly, the fruitful pastor will consider his audiences and speak appropriately to various age groups, but he will speak about this vital topic, because if he is not proactive in training, he will have to be reactive in counseling the crises which are far harder to deal with.

Confronting those who are living in sexual sin is not easy, but it must be done for the sake of the individual AND the church. The unavoidable truth that sinning believers cannot escape is in Galatians 6:8, "For he who sows to his flesh will of the flesh reap corruption, but he who sows to the Spirit will of the Spirit reap everlasting life." The word "corruption" could better be translated "ruin...decay...deterioration."[59] Over 25+ years of marriage counseling I can confidently say that 95% or more of the couples I see in crisis were having sex during dating and engagement. As a police chaplain I have responded to events where illicit sexual liaisons led to murder. Beyond the sin of the church members, there is great havoc created by pastors who are unfaithful to their wife and some even coming out as homosexual.[60]

Most important for this study of leadership is Paul's insistence that something should have been done in the Corinthian church. Paul does not address his exhortation about handling this sin to a specific leader or group of them, but clearly some structure and responsibility was active in the church

---

[59] Vincent, M. R. *Word Studies in the New Testament Volume 3*. McLean, Virginia: MacDonald Publishing, 1886, 1001.
[60] We have had two men in our fellowship of 65+ churches "come out" in the last 30 years. Thankfully, one of them eventually repented and died in fellowship with Christ. However, MUCH damage was done in the process.

when he told them to, "Purge out the old leaven" referring to the sexually sinful brother (1 Corinthians 5:7). In 14:40 he again implies leadership when he says, "Let all things be done decently and in order." No godly pastor can be aware of publicly known sexual sin and say with resignation, "There's nothing I can do about it, sigh." Matthew 18 gives us a process and several other passages including Titus 1:11, 2 Thessalonians 3:6, 14, 1 Corinthians 5:5-7, give us commands to condemn sin and to separate from unrepentant church members.

As with wrong doctrine, the fruitful pastor needs to grow in his **ability to see potential or actual sexual sin early** before it has rained down all the harm it can do when left unchecked. When I was a younger pastor, my wife and I had lunch with another pastoral couple. This man began talking about a book written by a friend about sexual fantasy. The thesis of the book was that sexual fantasy (in the mind) is inevitable and harmless. In fact, the author asserted that it is good because it allows an outlet for what otherwise might become physical sin. I was shocked, to say the least, and I tried to push back. However, this man was significant in my ministry life, and I was much less skilled in the Scripture and in observations of life at that time. A few years later, I was shocked again to find out he had been having an adulterous relationship for some time. If I heard such talk now (about sexual fantasy), I would immediately be concerned and I would confront the brother. This man's fall created huge waves, some of which are still lapping on the shore 30 years later.

Protecting the church from sexual sin means managing the children's and youth ministries with careful circumspection. There are many books and even whole ministries devoted to helping churches create an environment that dissuades the would-be molester from living out his evil behavior at church. The fruitful pastor will take this threat seriously. I have personally interacted with those whose children were not protected and fell victim to predators. It is easy to think that such things will not happen in 'our' church, but they can if precautions are not taken.

The local church should be a group of people who uphold righteousness—not out of prideful self-achievement, or to demonstrate a superior knowledge of the truth, but because it is best for the child of God, the church, and above all it honors the Savior.

Worship Authenticity

"The true worshipers will worship the Father in spirit and truth; for the Father is seeking such to worship Him" (John 4:23). This is the summary of the kind of worship a child of God should be offering Him. While we know that all obedience is received by God as worship (i.e., Hebrews 13:16, Philippians 4:18) there is also an imperative for the church of God to carry on certain mandates from Him as part of their regular gathering. The Apostle Paul emphasized this when he wrote to Timothy regarding the importance of prayer (1 Timothy 2:1-8), the ministry of the Word (1 Timothy 4:13), and to who could participate in teaching the whole church (2 Timothy 2:9-15) when it gathered. Elsewhere we read that God intends for His people to sing to each other (Colossians 3:16), to observe the Lord's Supper (1 Corinthians 11:23-34), to give of their possessions to the Lord's work (I Corinthians 16:1-2) and to use whatever gifts He has given them for the good of the whole church (1 Corinthians 12).

More could be said to fully enunciate the doctrine of church ministry when gathered, but the critical element of the oversight of worship (we will consider teaching/preaching separately even though the impact of that is worship through lives changed) is where I would like to direct your attention. In a protracted teaching on how the local church ought to function, we read this command to the enthusiastic, but not fully God-honoring, members of the church at Corinth, "How is it then, brethren? Whenever you come together, each of you has a psalm, has a teaching, has a tongue, has a revelation, has an interpretation. Let all things be done for edification" (1 Corinthians 14:26). Paul then concludes these detailed instructions with v. 40, "Let all things be done decently and in order." The flock of believers in a local church need their shepherd(s) to guide their activity so they will accomplish God's purposes for worship.

In my father's generation of conservative pastors, it was common to refer to the portion of the church service before the preaching as the "pre-service" or the "singing." It was either a practicality because people could not stand an hour of just preaching, or it was an accommodation for those who loved to sing. When my dad was a boy in the deep south, his church's service began with women singing while the men stood outside smoking. When it was time for preaching, someone would go out and tell the men to come in. The men would carefully tamp out their cigarettes and lay them in order on the sidewalk to be retrieved and finished after the sermon. Worship is not a "pre-service" nor just a fun time of singing for the musically inclined, it is to be "the fruit of our lips giving praise to His name" (Hebrews 13:15) and it needs to be treated with the same respect as all of God's commands.

The pastors of a local church should be "lead worshippers" whether they are on the platform or not. They should be seen in the congregation attentively participating in every part of the church service. Just as they are to ensure right doctrine, they also must ensure God-honoring worship. Even if one of the pastors dedicates part or all of his time to the worship aspect of the service, the senior or lead pastor must guide the development and implementation of the worship of God in "spirit and in truth." He does not have to personally lead the worship service unless that is one of his skills, but he does need to work with those who will participate in leading the worship through teaching, prayer, and discussion so that what they plan will enable the congregation to lift their heart and voice to God in confession, thanksgiving, and praise.

In my lifetime (I have attended church now for 68 years, having started when I was two weeks old) I have seen church worship services go from complete "insider" orientation, to complete "outsider" orientation, and back to an insider focus by many who rejected the "seeker" model and argue that the church is for the believer. In Paul's discussion of the miraculous gifts, which included speaking in other languages, he exhorted the Corinthians to be aware of how their activities would impact the "*unbeliever* or an uninformed person" (1 Corinthians 14:24 & 25 emphasis added). Tim Keller, who developed an incredibly fruitful church (and a series of church plants) in New York City, expressed the balance of focus in a local church worship service when he commented that church services should be "comprehensible" to the unbeliever. The error is when we seek to make them "comfortable."[61] I strongly agree.

The fruitful pastor will not abandon the needs of his flock but will keep in mind the needs of unbelievers who may be present in church. Some of those who will attend every week may indeed be unbelievers either on purpose or by accident (that is, they may not fully grasp their condition yet or be the children of believers who are forced to attend). Keller[62] offers key ideas on how to make the service comprehensible to the unbeliever:

Seek to worship and preach in the vernacular.

Explain the service as you go.

Directly address and welcome nonbelievers.

Consider using highly skilled arts in worship.

Celebrate deeds of mercy and justice.

---

[61]Keller, Timothy. *Center Church*. Grand Rapids: Zondervan, 2012, 304.
[62]Ibid., 304-305.

Present the sacraments so as to make the gospel clear.

Preach grace.

I will not comment on these principles except to say this in summary, everything in a worship service should be done in plain language. The pastor should model this and teach others who serve in worship leadership to do the same. Those who speak to the congregation during the service (i.e., welcome, music, announcement, preaching) should ask themselves if they are using words in such a way that everyone can grasp the full meaning. When they talk about events or the service itself, do they give enough information so that the newest person in the room can understand what is being said. The most important person in a worship service to do this is the preacher of God's Word. The shepherd sets the tone for all who stand up to speak. The pastor must train his people to be mindful of the unbeliever and Christians who are not fully engaged with the Lord or the church, not to pander to their desires but to enable them to grasp the truth and engage with God.

Ministry effectiveness

"Church the way it used to be" was the slogan on the banner attached to a building down the street from our facility. A congregation from a neighboring town purchased the building with a desire to replicate themselves. After renovations they began holding services. They also advertised that they used the King James Version of the Bible and sang from the hymnbook. About that same time, I attended a service at a similar church where the pastor used the identifier "old-fashioned" to describe himself and the church multiple times during the service. I was taken back to the expression of a Bible college history teacher who frequently quoted the preacher of Ecclesiastes saying, "What is the cause that the former days were better than these?"

While the goal of church ministry has not changed since Jesus gave the apostles their marching orders, the way that ministry is conducted has changed dramatically over the centuries. For anyone to assert that their church is superior (godlier?) because it is "old-fashioned" or "the way it used to be" is either arrogant or unstudied. It would be more informative if a church said, "We do church like it was done in the ____'s [fill in the decade]." We certainly do not do church like they did in the days of the Apostles. How do I know? Because churches today do not meet in the Temple or "house to house" ("house" churches notwithstanding) nor do they share all their possessions (Acts 2:45-46) for just a few examples. We also have no idea what their music sounded like[63], nor are we certain what the difference between a "hymn" and a "spiritual song" was, as instructed in Colossians 3:16, perhaps which is why the opinions on these matters are myriad.

We could fly over 2,000 years of church history and find a variety of types of church services and ministry activities which we no longer practice. We would hear a variety of ways to sing God's praise that would be foreign to our ears, but we would see the same Scripture read and taught, doctrines defended, and errant church practices corrected so that today we can confidently say we are accomplishing the same things that the true Church always has throughout the centuries; that is, making disciples of Christ who honor Him with godly lives.

Why should a church modify their methods of carrying out the non-changing mandate of Christ? Change is necessary because Christ's ministry needs to be contextualized to the people a church is trying to reach. "Sound contextualization means translating and adapting the communication and ministry of the gospel to a particular culture without compromising the essence and particulars of the gospel itself" (Keller, Center

---

[63] An AI assisted online search with this question, "What tone-scale was used in first century Jewish music" yielded an article that suggested the Jews used a 7-note scale in what we would call a minor key. However, neither secular nor sacred research can demonstrate with any certainty what ancient music was like. The one clue we have in the Bible is the names of the instruments in the Old Testament. However, we have no knowledge of what they sounded like nor what key they may have been made to play.

Church 2012). We expect a foreign missionary to learn the heart language and cultural norms of the people he is trying to reach. If they call the left hand the "dirty hand," he will not use it to eat his food in their presence. If all the women wear long skirts (as it was in Togo, W. Africa until recent years) then the female missionaries wear long skirts, always. Whatever is doable without compromising Bible truth, the faithful missionary does.

The problem we seem to have in the USA is thinking that everyone is an "American," so we all live and like the same things. This homogenized view of our culture causes pastors to see no need to adapt the ministry to their local culture. We expect those who walk through the church doors to adjust to whatever model we think is best. In contrast to this way of thinking, the fruitful pastor is consistently observing the society around his church. If the goal of a church includes making new disciples (and it must!) then the church will do ministry in a way that does not feel foreign to those people who need Christ.

Leading a local church to appropriate contextualization of the ministry is a significant challenge for many pastors. Whether music, styles of dress for those on the platform, service times and plans, facility design, or ministry programs, people like what they like and will often fight to keep it. When I came into one new ministry, the organ had an electronic fault and would make very loud intermittent noises. I did the research and found it would cost a fairly large sum of money not allotted in our tight budget to try and fix it. One older member said, "I'll pay for that repair, because I know what will happen if you get rid of the organ. You'll put drums on the platform!" The organ was unsavable, and he was long gone before we had a drummer!

Not all needed change is cultural in nature. Especially when entering a new ministry, a pastor may find unspiritual or immature Christians serving in roles that requires better. There can be staff members who develop problems and need to be removed. There are times when the church needs to grow in faith by giving to missionaries or other worthy endeavors.

Facilities and programs can need change due to deterioration and demographic shifts in the impact area. No matter how weighty the issue may be, change is often hard for many pastors and church members.

How does a pastor grow in leading for change?

First, he must have a **vision for needed change**. Some wise man said that a pastor should make a list of everything he believes needs change in his first year of a new ministry because he will soon become so comfortable with the way things are that he will no longer notice the rough spots. The fruitful pastor must be a student of culture AND of how well the church is accomplishing its mission of making disciples. There will always be room for improvement on this side of heaven. Sometimes the vision for change will come from a fellow elder or a church member who sees how ministry could be done better or add something that is not being done at all. The wise pastor does not run after every idea, but he does give them due consideration.

As a pastor begins to envision changes he believes are necessary, **he must go to God in prayer**. I attended a seminar by a pastor who was known for his MUCH praying. He changed my life when he said, "I don't like to pray, it's a lot of work, but there are a lot of things I want."[64] At that moment I thought of my burdens for change in the church I had come to pastor just five months prior, some of which were deeply spiritual in nature and seemed insurmountable. I went home and stepped up my prayer life and began to see God make changes directly as well as guiding our leaders and the whole church to make changes. Not only must a lead pastor himself pray, but as he begins to sense what needs to change, he prays with his fellow elders, deacons, and other leaders about the issues.

---

[64]Pastor Dee Duke from Jefferson Baptist Church, Jefferson, OR at a pastor's seminar.

A vital step in moving a church toward needed change is **teaching on themes that support change.** I am not advocating for topical sermons that enable the pastor to eisegete passages to accomplish anything he wants in a church. I *am* saying that there are Biblical mandates that encourage appropriate change. Most important is the theme of "mission" expounded from texts like 1 Corinthians 6:9-11 which tells us how great the transformation of the people in this church was. Realizing that I had an ex-homosexual in our church for the first time, I emphasized texts like this one and challenged people in their attitudes toward people who were very different from the average church member. I did not tell them about the church member for some time until I was ready to preach a short series on how believers grow and change. As part of that series, he shared a lengthy prepared testimony. The church responded with love, and I think their spiritual hearts and minds grew a bit in their ability to accept one another (Romans 15:7). Growing people to be **mission minded, not comfort driven,** is a huge step toward garnering unified change. Teaching on **cultural adaptation** from passages like 1 Corinthians 9 and Romans 14 is vital. We need to see Paul's example in such teaching and emulate it (1 Corinthians 11:1).

Another important **theme for change is excellence.** In Colossians we read, "Whatever you do, do it heartily, as to the Lord and not to men." The cousin of one of my leading church members visited our church one Sunday and gave him this feedback in an email, "It was a wonderful service with a life-affirming message, surrounded by fake flowers and brown spots." This man was a pastor who gave his input with a kind heart. While I knew our outdated décor and the remnants of an old audio system needed to change on the platform and the walls behind it, I was moving quite slowly to get it done...until I heard his impression of our service. I had grown comfortable while the culture around me moved on. One Sunday a first-time visitor reflected on the condition of the facility when she said, "I did not know if this [church] was still open." That is how rundown the exterior looked!

I taught often and directly both from the pulpit and in leadership meetings about the importance of excellence in our culture. Excellence is a moving target with the culture. I have sat on hard benches in an African church, which is excellent for them, because it is better than sitting on the ground! But that does not work in most of the USA. The fruitful pastor will take note of commercial facilities and offices that he frequents and the houses of his people and the tenor of the community, and from all this input he will develop a necessary level of excellence for his church.

God's **design of leadership** in the church is a theme that is hard to teach but must be communicated if the church would function well, especially when change is needed. I strongly subscribe to a collaborative model of leaders working together as a group to guide the congregation to decisions for ministry. My last church changed from a Pastor-and-deacons congregational model to an elder-led congregational government. We worked hard to teach, teach, teach, and discuss, discuss, discuss, before the vote to change our structure was unanimously approved. As part of that effort, we emphasized the importance of identifying spiritual leaders (elders) and then following their lead. Church members who think that congregational governance equals democracy (one man one vote, majority rules no matter how slim) need to learn that the goal of a church structure is to enable the body of believers to find God's will with due consideration to His leading through the elders.

The companion theme to teaching on leadership is **unity**. Church members must realize that it is their duty to work at maintaining the unity the Holy Spirit is trying to build (Ephesians 4:1-3). Self-seeking, sinful, comfort-loving, compassion-impoverished "saints" must be taught that their vision of the church is wrong. The church exists to glorify Christ by making disciples and that goal must drive the behavior and decisions of the leaders and all members of a local church. If that is true, unity will prevail.

With good vision, prayer, and teaching, the next step for creating change is **planting seed thoughts.** Our uncomfortable, worn-out pews needed to be exchanged for chairs but that would be a HUGE change for some people and a significant expense. For several years, at every opportunity, I talked about how great it would be to have flexible seating. This was mostly casual, one-on-one interaction meant to help others envision what I could see. After some time, we put a line item in the budget for interior design (our whole auditorium needed a significant rehab and upgrade). The designer helped us see what could be done in our worship room including how many chairs we would need and several ways they could be arranged. A couple more years passed and quite miraculously, from outside the church came a gift large enough for chairs and a complete repair and improvement of the worship area, *AND* the decision to change to chairs was unanimous!

Seed thoughts need to be planted with fellow leaders first. The fruitful pastor does not go around leadership to the congregation. Discussion and prayer that yield a unified desire among leaders is the vital starting point of accomplishing new things in a church. As seeds of change are planted, often they sprout up into new ideas from others who believe they thought them up! The fruitful pastor does not care who gets the credit, as long as God's work goes forward!

An important next step is **watching and listening for God's timing.** As I mentioned above, the interior design fee was approved, and the design was created, but we had no money to pay for the work and did not believe that it was the time for more debt or fundraising. I prayed, and I assume others did also, and God opened the windows of heaven. One of the prime ways that God's timing can be perceived is by the unity of the leadership and the membership. I do not subscribe to the belief that every decision must be 100% unified, but a definite consensus related to plans and decisions must be sought. I do believe that the effective pastor is always listening to see if the idea under discussion seems to be resonating positively with most of the people. If not, he goes back to the prayer closet and discussion table to refine the direction. Unity can be forced ("Well...I better vote yes because I don't want to be the holdup") but it does not yield fruitful ministry in the long run.

This brings us to an important quality of leadership which is **patience**. In my observation, most pastors generally have good vision for ministry, but sometimes they get in a hurry. When there is a temptation to rush, the fruitful pastor remembers that there are only two things he cannot do without in ministry: the Word of God and prayer. Everything else is flexible and God will provide in unique ways for various ministries in His time.

Fearfulness is the opposite but equally hazardous quality to impatience. The impatient pastor runs ahead of God's people and finds himself trying to pull them along where they are not ready to go. The fearful pastor realizes that some people will not like certain choices, so he does nothing in an effort to preserve what he thinks is peace. There will often be push-back on any change but that alone must not stop careful progress. When I came to my last church, I was criticized for standing in a different place in the foyer after church than the previous pastor while greeting people. Never mind that I did not do it on purpose. After a few things like that, it is not hard to see why some pastors stop trying to pursue progress. To pastor Timothy who seems to have struggled with the fear of man, Paul wrote, "For God has not given us a spirit of fear, but of power and of love and of a sound mind" (2 Timothy 1:7).

The fruitful pastor who pursues mission-driven change, with prayer, discussion, unity of leadership, and appropriate teaching, needs to trust God and graciously move forward by **asking for decisions on plans and ideas**. There comes a time when a decision must be made. I was asked to serve on the board of an organization with which I was very familiar. In our first meeting there were several issues discussed but there was no request for a decision. My hand went up and I said, "There is a need, right?" "Yes." "And we have the money?" "Yes." "And we all agree that this is the best way to meet the need?" "Yes." "Then I move..." and the decisions were made. I was dumbfounded at the lack of leadership. Leaders must lead, or nothing gets done.

There is a **spiritual gift of leadership.** Romans 12:8 refers to someone who "leads" meaning "To be over, to superintend, preside over."[65] Also, in 1 Corinthians 12:28 we see the gift of "administrations" from a root word meaning, "governing."[66] In 1 Timothy 5:17 Paul refers to two emphases of elders in a church, one of leading and another of teaching. It seems reasonable that taken together we would understand that some elders are gifted as leaders or managers and others are gifted as teachers. This is not to create categories or hierarchies among the elders but to recognize God's gift of both kinds of men to the local church. Some men use this reality to excuse themselves from leading the flock. If in fact there are other godly men who are willing and able to lead, that will indeed leave one or more men free to focus on the ministry of the Word. However, if no specially gifted men are present, the elders who remain must pick up the mantle of leadership. The tasks of a spiritual leader of God's flock must be accomplished by the men God has called to do so.

Fruitful local church ministry does not happen just by teaching God's Word. The pastor who would accomplish God's work must also lead in conjunction with other leaders and the congregation. Effective ministry is the result of spiritual leadership. While leading can be challenging, the fruitful pastor

---

[65]Thayer, Joseph Henry. *Thayer's Greek English Lexicon of the New Testatment.* Grand Rapids, Michigan: Zondervan, 1974, 539.
[66]Ibid., 364.

will embrace his God-given role and grow into the well-rounded shepherd God has called him to be.

We began our study of growth as a pastor considering God's use of the term "elder" to describe spiritual maturity as the key quality of those who lead His people. We worked through a very robust explanation of how spiritual growth happens and why it is vitally important for the man who would be a fruitful pastor. We have considered how a spiritual leader must be growing in the work of pastoral care through the public and private communication of God's Word. Then we turned to the other half of pastoral ministry and considered the mandate of leadership and management in the local church and how a man can grow in this vital area.

In our final chapter I want to direct your attention to some common activities that vocational pastors walk through and consider how they might be avenues of growth. We often measure activities in how much time they will take, how important they seem to be, or what they will accomplish, but I want to challenge you to consider how certain pastoral opportunities might contribute to your growth as a servant of God. If your goal is to be fruitful for your Savior and Chief-shepherd, I would encourage you to take a fresh look at these common aspects of pastoral ministry.

Questions/Ideas for Application

Make a list of the changes you believe your church needs.

   Categorize them

- Doctrinal alignment
- Moral purity
- Worship ministry
- Delayed maintenance
- Cultural connection
- Mission enhancement

Commit to praying about these needs daily

Prayerfully **prioritize** the needs

Evaluate what you have done to move your church toward the needed changes.

Evaluate what you need to do more of, to move toward the changes (see the ideas in this section on how to lead).

Add your **top concerns** and plans to your **prayer list.**

Choose several leadership actions and **move** toward the needed changes, keeping an open heart and hand to allow God to modify your plans along the way.

Chapter 13

UNDER-USED COMPONENTS OF GROWTH

When one of my daughters was about 12 years old, she decided to bake a cake after school. As I walked in the door from work that afternoon, I saw the cake sitting on the counter looking somewhat less than the picture of perfection. The recipe she used was lying open on the counter. Being a fairly competent baker myself, I read the recipe and noticed some ingredients and processes that I thought might have been unknown to her. As she talked about her frustration with the poor result of her efforts, I asked her if she had done this, or included that, to which she replied in a disgusted tone, "No." Baking recipes have been tested and refined until the desired product is predicable. The ingredients and their quantities are required, not optional, and when one is left out, the results are usually disappointing.

God has laid out a recipe for pastoral growth which we have been considering at length. Most of the ingredients we have discussed are fairly obvious but there are three other components that I see in the process of growth which sometimes are not recognized, are lightly practiced, are even purposefully avoided by some men, resulting in stagnation, frustration, and less fruitful ministry.

Accepting Invitations to Serve

God puts desires, abilities, and experiences into a man's heart and life which He uses to direct him to a place of pastoral service. When he finds that place of service through the call of God's people and the peace of the Holy Spirit, he settles down into the rhythm of that ministry and does his best to please the

Lord by shepherding the flock. I think it is fair to assume that in this, the men of the first century were not different from the men of the 21st century. We read about the ministry assignments of Paul, Barnabas, Timothy, Titus, and more as the Body of Christ was first being formed, but perhaps we do not consider how they thought about their evolving roles.

The Apostle Paul spent his first three years as a believer in Damasus. Eventually we find him in Antioch via a stopover in Jerusalem and from there sent with Barnabas to strike out into the unknown and be the first missionaries. Might they have wanted to settle down and build the church in one of these places? Paul told Timothy to stay put in Ephesus and develop the church. Maybe Timothy liked the nomadic life with Paul and staying put was a sacrifice, especially with a church that needed serious correction. Paul told Titus that he was going to send Artemas to him. Did Artemas have a say in that? Epaphroditus was sent by Paul to the Philippian church. Did he want to go?

My point is simply this, these men appear to have put themselves at God's disposal to do whatever was needed when He called them through various people and circumstances. Epaphroditus valued His service to God more than his own life (Philippians 2:30). Timothy had to do the hard work of earning respect (1 Timothy 4:12). The Apostle Paul endured untold hardship because of his missionary zeal (2 Corinthians 11:22-33). Instead of answering God's calls to specific ministry activities, they could have responded as this man who left the ministry for selfish reasons, "Demas has forsaken me, having loved this present world" (2 Timothy 4:10).

In my work as the Executive Director of a network of Baptist churches, I have been in contact with many men who were seeking a pastorate, some for the first time and others sensing a transition was needed. I always ask, "Where would you like to be?" The sentiment of the reply is always the same even if the words vary, "Anywhere the Lord wants me." When I describe our churches that need pastors, the response is usually something like, "Well... not there." I would say (tongue in cheek), it seems that men are looking for a well-functioning church of 200 members offering a good health insurance plan. I have only had one man in eight years willing to investigate an opportunity to go to a struggling church and help them rebuild.

Please understand, there is no bitterness here. I know there are empty pulpits all over the country and I know I do not have special knowledge of the calls of God to men for pastoral work so that I might know exactly where they belong. As I said when I started this section, every man has desires, abilities, and experiences that help shape his service for God. Sometimes these things surface in the form of personal ambitions to do a particular ministry or to serve in a certain geography or setting. Such pursuits are not wrong *unless they stop a man from answering God's call* to a kind of ministry or a place of service beyond his ambition or desire for comfort. Human beings tend to "feather their nest," that is, they like to make the circumstances of life as comfortable and predictable as possible. That in and of itself is not wrong. In a local church a pastor wants to get acquainted with his people and settle into a rhythm for the activities of life and ministry. Such lifestyle structure is good, *unless it keeps a man from answering God's call* to a work God may have for him.

I am not advocating for frequent "ship jumping," that is, moving from church to church whether to escape difficulty or pursue a larger and purportedly more significant platform. Pastors should not "climb the ladder" to get to the top of their "career." The network of churches I served values long-term pastorates with some men serving a single congregation for 40+ years. What I am challenging you to consider is this—God may need you to accept an invitation to a place that is unknown to you or uncomfortable for you. It might be smaller or bigger than you like. It might be far away from family or too close to them. It might be in a setting in which you do not feel at home, whether urban or rural. There might be serious problems needing resolution or an extreme need to contextualize the ministry after years of stagnation.

I am challenging you to consider that **God might be calling you to *grow* into a greater level of pastoral fruitfulness through the call to a ministry that seems beyond your ability in some way.** This is based in the principle of James 1 where God allows you to "fall into" a situation that is hard in order to cause you to cling to him as you patiently follow His Word while He makes you more like Christ and grows you into a more capable shepherd than when you started, and in the process enhances the ministry of one of His local churches.

After 15 years in an urban setting, God very clearly called me to a suburban setting in an area far from where I wanted to be. On the candidate weekend, I learned that the church was seriously divided over a personnel issue. Not to mention that the church had a dominating deacon who was very invested on one side of that issue and many others. The church was ripe for a debilitating explosion, and I had no experience with such a situation. One of the pastors in our network was known for seeking out such churches. He led several of them out of difficulty back to productive ministry, but I did not believe I was that man. Through a series of life and ministry circumstances (like a divided church calling me with a near unanimous vote) I believed this was God's next assignment for my wife and me.

God helped me lead through issues with which I had no experience to rebuild the unity of the church. Over the next 15 years, we remodeled the facility, restructured the governance, rewrote the constitution, re-formed the worship and services, and saw God make new disciples and enliven some who had been complacent. Please believe me when I say this is not a humble brag, rather I would have you understand that **I had to step out in faith** going where I did not want to go, believing God would enable me to lead this divided flock back to fruitful ministry. When I stepped out, God led me, taught me, strengthened me, and grew me to be the man He needed to rebuild a floundering flock.

How might a man recognize the call of God from one ministry to another? First, God calls through His people. A man might feel like his ministry is completed in a certain field, but if no one is asking him to move, God is not calling. If God has disquieted a man and if the Holy Spirit sparks an interest in his heart, when a request comes, a pastor should consider how God has enabled him (all men have strengths and weaknesses) and what the ministry who is inquiring needs in their next leader. As I met with the pulpit committee of the church I just mentioned, and as I interacted with the church, I realized that they needed a leader who saw their potential that could be developed with much change. I sensed that I was that kind of man and eventually believed I was the man.

One of the absolute keys to all ministry change is humility. The man who seeks or welcomes the opportunity to move to a bigger and "better" ministry simply because it seems more significant or will pay a bigger salary needs to quash his pride and put his life back on the altar of service. Philippians 4:6-7 applies to pastoral moves just as much as every other Christian life issue. The fruitful pastor will pray and seek the peace of God as his rule in all these considerations.

There may be times when a man senses the disquieting of God and is presented with an interesting opportunity which he desires to investigate. Discussions should be had, and interviews undertaken—all with prayer and motivational examination. In such a process God will either knit hearts together or keep them apart.

Above all, such movements must be undertaken seriously with much prayer and consultation with more mature experienced pastors. A pastor cannot make such changes without due consideration for how it will impact the church he leaves and the one to which he might go, not to mention how it impacts his family. In a particular time of disquieting, after a dozen or more years at one church, I was asked to meet with the leaders of another church. They bought me dinner and explained why they thought I should be their next pastor. I thought their reasoning was sound and I saw how I could meet their needs. I went home and told my family, whereupon one of my high school aged girls said, "You just go ahead and go." Meaning, *we are not going anywhere.* I believed this was God speaking to me, so I withdrew from their consideration. (And in retrospect, it was the right decision.)

There is much prayer, wisdom, and patience needed in finding God's leading from one ministry to the next. I do want to stress my main point in this section again, God may call a man to a place and group that is extremely challenging for one reason or another. That should not keep a pastor from following God's lead because He will use it to grow that man into a more effective servant who will accomplish God's will for that time and place.

There is a **second aspect to accepting God's invitations** to ministry which is equally important for the pastor who wants to be fruitful for Christ. The comfort we desire and build in life and ministry can not only keep us from accepting the call to a church, but it can also keep us from accepting a call to add something to our ministry plate. Every pastor, whether a lead elder or a paid staff member, has a number of regular responsibilities. From time to time, requests will come from outside the church to add something to that list. The youth pastor may be asked to help plan an area-wide retreat, one of the pastors may be asked to be a board member of an associated ministry organization, a civic club may ask a man to join; the possibilities are myriad.

I fully realize that time is limited, and priority choices must be made, but one of the factors that should be considered when these opportunities arise is **pastoral growth.** God may be calling a man to stretch into a new role which He will empower.

I assume that one of the major pushbacks would be time. How can a man take on an extra ministry activity without impinging on current duties? If the invitation truly is from God, then God will give an increase of productivity or make time available to accomplish those needful things in some unexpected way. Best of all, God will use the whole experience to grow a man into a more fruitful pastor!

In my first church, where I was an associate pastor of youth and music (old school title, I know) I was asked by a church member to join the volunteer fire department. That sounded like a fun hobby to me, so I agreed.[67] I started learning how to be a fire fighter and I took the opportunity to take an Emergency Medical Technician (EMT) class. I responded to fires of many sizes, car accidents, all kinds of medical situations, and saw death from many causes. I did CPR and made death notifications when it did not work. I responded to calls involving our own church people. I saw life at its rawest. I hung out with the other fire fighters and learned much about relating to men, especially those who are unsaved. I made stupid mistakes and learned lessons in humility. Not only did I grow during those years, but later I realized that God was preparing me to become an emergency services chaplain for police, fire, medical organizations, and more in several jurisdictions. Through these I learned about life in ways nothing else could have taught me. I saw a few people saved and baptized and saw my belief in God having the ONLY answers for life's greatest calamities become rock solid.

I could have said I did not have time for the fire department. In addition to being a very active ministry with a church of 450 congregants by the time I left, I had a young family at home. I could have begged off by asserting that I had no skill or background. I could have been fearful of failure and

---

[67]Today the training requirements of this kind of work today are VASTLY greater and might not be possible for the average pastor. In that day it worked for me.

found an excuse for not saying yes. By God's grace I did say yes, and my ability to handle crisis, to understand life and death, and to shepherd my people grew immensely.

Years later, accepting the call to a divided church was just a first step in a process which enabled me to grow exponentially in my last pastorate. Over my 15-year ministry, there were three men who caused significant difficulties for me, and I had to work through those challenges with my leaders and the whole church. This church was of a size to underwrite and encourage my graduate education, which I had desired for some time. They were able to send me to several foreign countries to serve alongside our missionary partners. All of these experiences helped me grow in my ability to communicate God's Word in various settings and enlarged my understanding of His work in the world. What I did not know was that God was preparing me for the role I now fill in leading a group of churches in our joint ministry and assisting pastors with many of the very challenges and opportunities I faced over four decades of pastoral work.

One opportunity that often comes to local church leaders is the invitation to serve on a ministry board. It could be a youth camp, a Christian school, a mission organization, Bible college, seminary, or a church network. This kind of service takes time and effort—the two things that always seem to be in short supply. The fruitful pastor will prayerfully consider such requests because they have an impact on the organization, *AND* on him. It is easy to understand that a man's service on a board will profit that ministry, but it also benefits the man. Such service brings him into a working relationship with other good men whose influence can strengthen his church leadership. Becoming more aware of the greater work of Christ can lift a man's eyes and heart to lead his church to a broader vision of the Lord's work.

One of my most unique ministry requests in recent years came from a counseling pastor at a large church which is not part of my network. Because we share a belief in Biblical

Counseling, and because I had lost my first wife to cancer, this man asked me to speak on grief at an event. Subsequently he received a request from a church member who wanted to have a chaplain for his business which employed 125 people. My friend could not do it but knowing my experience as a chaplain asked me if I would be interested. This restaurant was located an hour from where I live but the opportunity was so rare that I met with the owner. As we discussed the possibilities, I offered to train the pastor who would coming to our church in the town where his restaurant was located. He agreed and we set things in motion. We had a subsequent meeting where I introduced the pastor to the restaurant owner. The first time the local pastor came to the restaurant, he led a man to the Lord and the chaplaincy was off and running, and I never served there in person myself! I could have just as easily said this need was outside my responsibility and too far from my home to be viable.

I have a friend who recently retired from the most elite military unit in our country, if not the world. As we talked once about the training, he said it is designed to see how men perform under circumstances that are uncomfortable, because (as he said from 20+ years of experience) *combat is always uncomfortable*! Ministry is often uncomfortable, even when we have done it for a long while. I still get nervous before preaching, I often feel out of my depth in counseling, and it is not uncommon to have a knot in my stomach at leadership meetings. But I do not avoid these things, nor do I avoid accepting God's calls to ministries I may have never done before because I know God will guide and empower my surrendered life. He will accomplish His work through me, and in the process, grow me up to serve Him more and better in the future.

Cultivating Relationships for Growth

I cannot imagine what vocational ministry would have been like without five and a half years with a mentor pastor. As I was graduating from Bible college, pastors from two churches came seeking a youth and music pastor. I was just wise enough to see that one of them was looking for a man who could hit the ground running and the other wanted to train a co-worker. I accepted the second man's invitation and became the first full-time associate pastor ("staff member" in today's terminology) in a church of 250 that grew to 450 while I was there. There was no formal mentoring or discipleship plan. In fact, the word "mentor" was not used in the church setting in those days, but my Pastor *definitely* mentored me. We talked every day that we were at the church together. He taught me to receive critical input from people by considering their whole life and background. He taught me how to communicate with the church to evoke participation. He shared as much as he could from several ministry boards on which he served so I could learn how the broader church world worked.

He criticized, complimented, exhorted, encouraged, and directed my work until he pushed me out of the nest by recommending me to a small mission church as their second pastor. But his mentoring was not done, it just subsided into a more casual relationship. As a supported missionary from his church, he invited me to speak and stay in touch with the people I loved very much. In going to a single-pastor church, I felt ready for the challenge because my mentor had exposed me to and educated me about all aspects of the local church. He made sure that I was at every deacon board and building committee meeting. In addition to being completely responsible for the youth and music ministries, I baptized, preached, married, buried, led communion, got in and out of trouble, made mistakes, and had successes. I am still friends with people from that era and have done ministry with them in various ways over the ensuing decades.

When I began vocational ministry, *I did not know what I did not know.* I realize the over-simplification in that statement and its possible over-use, but the truth stands—for me and, in my opinion, every man entering vocational ministry for the first time. The epitome of this statement would be its application to the men who Jesus chose to be His partners. We have no idea what they expected when they, "Left their nets and followed Him" (Matthew 4:20), but I do not think it an overstatement to say that what they got was different than what they anticipated. Of course, Jesus knew exactly how things would go, and He was prepared to lead them along until He deemed them ready to send out on their own.

Jesus trained the 12 and they trained others. Paul trained several men including Timothy who was instructed to train others. Acquila and Priscilla helped train Apollos who did not know what he did not know (Acts 18:24-28)! The desire to be a spiritual leader (placed there by God) propels a man toward pastoral work, but to be effective, he needs to be prepared in the understanding and proclamation of God's truth, and in the leadership and management of God's house. The normal path for a young man aspiring to ministry used to be to leave his church and move near the seminary or Bible College he would attend. Even with a good formal education (which includes internships in some schools), a man in his first ministry does not know all he needs to know. There is much knowledge, wisdom, and skill to be gained from a mature man who serves as what we usually call a "mentor."

Mentoring

"Imitate me, just as I also imitate Christ" (1 Corinthians 11:1). With this uncomfortable command, Paul transmitted Christ's plan for the perpetuation of the Body of Christ to a new generation. Imitate (NKJV, NASB), "follow" (KJV), "follow my example" (NIV), literally, "mimic what one sees someone else doing."[68] When Jesus began selecting the men who would

---

[68]Brown, Colin. *The New International Dictionary of New Testament Theology*. Edited by Colin Brown. Vol. 1. Grand Rapids, MI: Zondervan, 1975, 490.

become the apostles, He asked them to "follow" Him, literally to "go somewhere with someone...and according to this word's metaphorical use, to following His opinion."[69] Jesus trained those who would spread His gospel by personal teaching, observation, and interaction.

The word "mentor" comes from Greek mythology where it was the name of a god who helped to raise a child for a friend. A more modern dictionary defines the term as, "A person in a company, college, or school who trains and counsels new employees or students, to advise or train someone."[70] The root idea simply being that a mentor is a more mature, experienced, skillful, and usually older person helping someone less mature and experienced or skillful to be successful in life and work. In their excellent work, *The Leadership Baton*, the authors make a fascinating observation, "A chapter on church-based mentoring wouldn't have been necessary a hundred years ago. People in that era would not have called it mentoring. They would have talked about an *apprentice* who learned alongside a *craftsman*—a mode of training...so commonplace as to hardly be worth mentioning."[71] Spiritually, a mentor is a skilled spiritual leader who pours into a novice through a close personal and professional relationship that is long-term in nature, a sort of "apprenticeship" that results in an aspiring pastor becoming a fruitful shepherd.

The vital importance of mentoring for pastoral development lies in the reality that there is no training like on-the-job training, especially for ministry. While a college or seminary can impart the tools for gaining a correct

---

[69] Brown, Colin. *The New International Dictionary of New Testament Theology*. Edited by Colin Brown. Vol. 1. Grand Rapids, MI: Zondervan, 1975, 481.
[70] Lindberg, Christine A., ed. *Oxford College Dictionary*. New York, New York: Putnam and Sons, 2002, 844.
[71] Forman, Rowland, Jeff Jones, and Bruce Miller. *The Leadership Baton*. Grand Rapids: Zondervan, 2004, 99.

understanding of the Scripture and how to communicate it faithfully, it cannot create the pressure of preaching to a congregation with varying needs and intellectual abilities week by week. With the right guidance from a skillful mentor, that pressure will cause an apprentice to refine his ways of presenting the Word so that he becomes an increasingly effective preacher. Similar examples could be given from every aspect of pastoral leadership. The knowledge gained in the classroom (or online, or in private study of academic/theological works) needs to be exercised, practiced, and honed under the tutelage of a skillful mentor. The seminary I attended requires a significant internship for those in the Master of Divinity program.

    The very best way for man entering vocational ministry to be mentored is to **seek a relationship** with a lead pastor who is not only willing but eager to **mentor** the novice. Being a pastor is WAY more than preaching, and even preaching on a regular basis is a greater challenge than it seems. Somehow, some way, every man entering vocational ministry needs to pray for and seek an opportunity to serve under and with a mature man. Yes, I said "under." Just because a man is an aspiring elder does not mean he is one even though he might be paid full-time to do pastoral work. The young man just out of school needs to find someone he can learn from and collaborate with and be protected by as he grows into a spiritual leader in his own right.[72]

    I met a missionary doctor who trains surgeons in the USA when not in a foreign country. I learned something that shocked me about surgeons. They learn how to perform surgery on the job with a teacher doing actual surgery. The time after formal medical education is called "residency." They do not go from classroom to career without it. This concept has been picked up in recent years for the pastorate. After a man completes his education, he is taken in by a church for a couple

---

[72] Not every Senior or Lead pastor wants to mentor an associate. I mentored a man in his first vocational pastoral position. His pastor literally walked by while we were chatting online and did not even say "Hi".

of years with a mentor pastor who is focused on giving the resident practical training with a goal of sending him out to a pastorate of some kind. While we might all agree that two years isn't enough, it is a very good start which a man can follow up with other mentors and coaches.

Coaching

The concept and practice of "coaching" is an even more contemporary phenomenon than mentoring, which began primarily in the business world. The word "coach" is from the name of a town (Coach) in Hungary where horse-drawn carriages were manufactured. Coaching was, "The process of transporting an individual from one place to another."[73] Unlike business coaching models that are only concerned with "carrying" a worker to more productivity or results, most Christian coaching experts would agree with Ogne and Roehl's concept of "transformissional coaching" which asserts that ministry and mission should "flow from the inside out."[74] They would agree with Thomas and Wood, who say that genuine Christian coaching is, "effective discipleship with leadership training."[75]

Coaching is an activity done at a greater distance than mentoring with those who need assistance in one or more aspects of ministry. Coaching assumes that the leader being assisted is capable in general but is challenged by a particular hurdle(s). Coaching involves caring about the leader *and* the Lord's work. The effective coach will listen carefully to understand what the leader might be missing in the spirituality of his approach to ministry and/or in his manner of carrying out

---

[73] Thomas, Scott, and Tom Wood. *Gospel Coach.* Grand Rapids: Zondervan, 2012, 24.
[74] Ogne, Steve, and Tim Roehl. *Transformissional Coaching.* United States: Missional Challenge Publishing, 2019, 2i.
[75] Thomas, Scott, and Tom Wood. *Gospel Coach.* Grand Rapids: Zondervan, 2012, 38.

plans and decisions. From these observations, the coach asks questions to cause the leader to think along lines that may have been missed. Ogne and Roehl call this "pulling out" what God is doing in people rather than the "pouring in" of mentoring.[76] The value in this approach is that the coach is causing the leader to think and integrate his knowledge and experience and depend on God's Word and prayer to make decisions or to create the action plan to which God is leading him. This sets up the pastor for future success by enabling him to use the same process on his own.

One of the avenues of coaching we are hearing a lot about currently is in regard to new church planters. Generally, it is younger, less experienced men with great desire and energy who are becoming lead church planters. The reality of shepherding a church that is yet being formed presents many challenges and makes the use of an experienced coach an incredibly wise choice. The average pastor can also benefit from coaching, as the pastorate usually brings its own set of problems, in God's providence, each one a little larger than the last. The benefit of a sympathetic listener who can guide the leader to consider new ways to look at a problem cannot be overstated.

Humility

The words "humble" and "humility" are used 13 times in the New Testament. Humility is a virtue while pride is the opposite vice. I realize that I did not tell you something new just now. So, I ask, why is it so hard for a man who wants to be a pastor, or one who is already serving, to seek a mature experienced brother who can be a mentor or coach? 1 Timothy 3:6 specifically identifies pride as a potential and dangerous weakness in the man who would be or who is a spiritual overseer. The wise man who spoke the Proverbs may have put his finger on part of the problem, "A man who isolates himself

---

[76]Ogne, Steve, and Tim Roehl. *Transformissional Coaching.* United States: Missional Challenge Publishing, 2019, 27.

seeks his own desire; He rages against all wise judgment. A fool has *no delight in understanding, But in expressing his own heart*" (Proverbs 18:1-2). In my experience, either as a man or as a gifted shepherd, my heart's desire is to figure out the answers by myself. I want to create the best plans—by myself. I do not want to lean on others for wisdom—and that is sinful pride!

1 Corinthians 12 teaches us that in the Body of Christ there are many kinds of spiritual gifts given to people for the benefit of all. It specifically says that one member of the Body cannot say that he or she does not need the rest of the Body. Do we really think that only applies to "lay" Christians within the local church? Or perhaps it only applies to churches as a whole helping one another? Or maybe, just maybe, it applies to everyone in the Body of Christ, including pastors! Make no mistake, we need each other, at some times more than others. The fruitful pastor will not hesitate to seek help from his brothers in the Lord's work.

Mark Wingfield, former pastor, and publisher of the Baptist Global News made this comment about pastors, **"Of all the things I've learned** through a few decades of mentoring young writers and pastors, one predictor of success stands out above all. This one thing rises above raw talent, education, or privilege — all of which may play a role in a person's success. That thing is having **a teachable spirit."**[77] The man who wants to be fruitful in the work of making disciples of Christ through the local church will seek and receive help from mature men because he cares more for the God-honoring results than he does his own esteem.

Men who have served for several years in vocational ministry should consider having mentors and coaches in their life. I am in no way suggesting that every man who serves as a

---

[77]Wingfield, Mark. "Opinion." *Baptist News Global.* October 21, 2021. https://baptistnews.com/article/the-one-thing-that-most-predicts-a-pastors-success/.

vocational pastor must have a teacher to whom they are constantly accountable. Rather, I am suggesting that they should be asking questions like these, "In what aspect of pastoral work do I need to improve?" "Do I see my strengths and weaknesses clearly?" "Am I striving to be the most fruitful pastor I can be, or am I just getting by to collect a paycheck?" "What mature brother do I seek out to get help with my challenges?" This kind of honest review can be painful and humbling, but remember, humility is the virtue!

Coaching can be as simple as having a man or men on whom you can call with a question. This is one of the aspects of my role as director of a network of churches. Men call and tell me their situation and we discuss factors that they should consider as they seek a path to move forward. Often what is needed is simply a different way of looking at things or a Biblical principle(s) enunciate that the pastor had not yet considered. Coaching can be a 'one-off' conversation, sometimes with a follow-up as needed. I have mentor/coach relationships with several men who found me in various ways. They are each doing effective ministry in different arenas but also feel like they need some outside perspective on various issues from time to time. They have different needs for input and encouragement, and we spend varying amounts of time together.

One of the important ways to use a coach or mentor is to ask for resources in the area of need. While the coach can give some input, a book, podcast, or similar resource can enable a man to dive deeper in an area of concern. If a man is respected and fruitful enough for you to seek his counsel for life and ministry, he can probably direct you to other helps you may not be familiar with. This in turn can lead to other coaching relationships, in essence, through those resources. A man who has written extensively on a particular aspect of theology or pastoral activity, he can be a mentor through his writings or recordings of teaching.

Another way to receive coaching is by **continuing education**. That is a broad term for conferences, retreats, and even formal academic work. A fruitful pastor needs to pursue input which can enhance his skill along two paths. The first is the known area of deficit. Because I am known as a counselor, I get inquiries about where to get counseling training. I am glad that men come to a place where they realize they need more ability to use the Scriptures to help their people. Similarly, a man might seek a greater understanding of a particular aspect of theology, or to develop as a communicator of God's Word. Every aspect of pastoral work can improve through learning from others who are several steps ahead in maturity and ability. I have benefited greatly from completing a master's degree and recently a Doctor of Ministry degree. I would say that with every class I took, the Lord caused me to see how the lessons learned directly applied to some current aspects of ministry.

I would also like to appeal to another result of continuing education which is receiving **input that was not specifically sought**. I come back to an earlier premise slightly modified which is this, you do not always know what you *need to know*. Many pastors develop a favorite area of study and teaching which can lead to pursuing education in some form about that topic. I have certainly done this myself in regard to Biblical Counseling and emergency service chaplaincy. This is good and ought to be done. But there also should be some opportunity for the Lord to nudge a man's learning and growth in ways he may not have known were needed.

This has happened to me at events planned by my network (long before I was the director!). Earlier I referred to some teaching on prayer that I did not know I desperately needed. That happened at a regularly scheduled one-day pastor's conference. Another time I went to a seminar on Biblical Creationism taught by Ken Ham. I expected to learn a few things and be reinforced in my understanding of the early chapters of Genesis, but I unexpectedly learned about witnessing to this "post-Christian" generation. I am not encouraging you to throw wisdom out the window and just choose conferences randomly, but I am encouraging you to be open to God's input that might come through events you consider less important. Above all, "Listen to counsel and receive instruction, That you may be wise in your latter days" (Proverbs 19:20).

I called this section, **"Cultivating Relationships for Growth,"** because doing a Google search for "pastoral mentor" is probably not the best way to find one. A good mentor will be someone with whom you share doctrinal alignment and for whom you have respect toward his effectiveness in ministry. My opinion is that this is best found in a network or association of churches with whom you fellowship regularly. In my ministry lifetime, many new Christian affinity groups have emerged for pastors. Think of large pastoral gatherings with serious teaching targeted at a particular doctrinal area or broadly on how pastors should lead their church. I am not against these events or their publications or the fellowship that they engender. However, what I believe is needed is sustainable friendships with other pastors with whom they can consistently interact over the years of their vocational service.

This kind of **relationship** comes best from **regional denominational fellowships**. Alas, many pastors are like the church members who frustrate them. Those members who are the last in the door, first out, and often absent from church services. Then, when problems occur, they are mad at the pastor for not knowing how much help they needed. One of the staff pastors in one of our network churches was asked to resign, thankfully, not for any of the common sinful reasons we hear about often, but it was still quite painful for him. His words to me were along this line, "I wanted to reach out for help, but I had not been connected much with the network, so I felt embarrassed to ask." So, he did not ask for help, which might have prevented his difficulty.

The **bottom line** is this, do not suffer alone. There is no glory for a pastor to go down in flames—alone. Building relationships for growth and encouragement will bring blessing to your soul and more effective ministry for you and your church.

Resting in God's encouragement

Thank you for sticking with me through my musing on pastoral growth. I sincerely hope you have been informed and encouraged in your life and ministry. I pray that you have learned some things that will enable the work of Christ to move forward through your work in the place God has assigned to you. I could never have imagined how my life in vocational ministry would turn out. I was so fearful of what complete surrender of my will to the Lord would mean. If I had known then what I know now...I would have surrendered sooner and gotten more years of this wonderful life. I could go on at length about the trials and challenges, but I want to end my thoughts with two empowering promises which I have watched God fulfill repeatedly in my life and ministry.

The first promise is one I discovered early in my surrendered walk. I was living the student life in Bible college and this promise was an encouragement, but I did not have the ability to see it working out significantly until I walked a while with the Lord in vocational ministry. In Mark 10 we read of an interchange between Jesus and a rich man which ended with Jesus telling the man, "One thing you lack: Go your way, sell whatever you have and give to the poor, and you will have treasure in heaven; and come, take up the cross, and follow Me" (v. 21). The man rejected this challenge and walked away, to which Jesus replied, "How hard it is for those who have riches to enter the kingdom of God!" (vs. 23). The disciples were watching this exchange, and Peter could not help but comment, "See, we have left all and followed You" (v. 28). With what might be a little bit of arrogance and a bit of quandary, Peter is concerned to know how his sacrifice will be compensated. To which Jesus replied with an incredible promise, "Assuredly, I say to you, there is no one who has left house or brothers or sisters or father or mother or wife or children or lands, for My sake and the gospel's, who shall not receive a hundredfold now in this time--houses and brothers and sisters and mothers and children and lands, with persecutions--and in the age to come, eternal life" (v. 29-30).

Do not fear, friend, I am not a health and wealth preacher, nor do I believe in a so-called "10-fold" payback guarantee as some do. Rather, simply put, *Jesus promises to take care of His servants*. If accepting his call to ministry requires sacrifice, He promises to make it up to those who serve Him. He does not tell us to make sacrifices *TO GET* His care, nor does He promise how or when He will care for us. This promise is akin to the teaching in 2 Corinthians 8-9 which is summarized in v. 9:8, "God is able to make all grace abound toward you (who willing give your money to His work), that you, always having all sufficiency in all things, may have an abundance for every good work." In other words, when we willingly give to the Lord, He makes certain that we can continue to give, just as the widow gave her oil and flour and it never ran out (1 Kings 17).

When I accepted the call to be an associate pastor, the compensation included living in a one-room apartment in the church and using the church kitchen for our cooking. My wife and I knew it was a sacrifice, but we did not care, we were in the Lord's work! It was not more than six months till we were able to get an apartment, then a house, then a bigger house all according to our needs. We lived some distance from our parents so when our second birth came along with twins, the church gave us a LAVISH shower and the ladies of the church came to help my wife four days a week for six months, because we had given up family to follow the Lord's call.

After 20+ years we were living in a parsonage with debt and no equity. I accepted the call to a church which I spoke about earlier as not being where we wanted to go nor was the ministry something we wanted to tackle. But we went with a joyful commitment to Christ and 15 years later left that ministry with no debt and substantial equity which has only increased to this day. God did this with several miracles which I will write about in another work, suffice it to say that the glory goes to Him for keeping His promise and blessing us beyond what we deserved. I offer only these two simple examples to challenge you to follow Christ, knowing that He has promised to care for you.

The **second encouraging promise** comes through the Apostle Peter in the same passage in which he gives the elders a summary job description. This promise, which is for all believers, has special significance for those who lead the Body of Christ. "Therefore, humble yourselves under the mighty hand of God, that He may exalt you in due time, casting all your care upon Him, for He cares for you" (1 Peter 5:6-7). This promise is very similar to the one spoken by Jesus in Mark 10 and could be paraphrased like this: when we make a sacrifice for Christ, He repays our kindness, sometime in the future. The difference here is that this promise is focused on how we conduct ourselves as believers.

On first blush, some would interpret this promise as a reference to heaven someday when we will receive reward(s) for the way we lived for Christ during our earthly sojourn. While that may be part of the meaning, I see more than eternity in this promise. Peter emphasized that future reward when he told the elders that there would be a special crown for them in heaven. Also, v. 5 relays the basis of this promise, namely that God graces the humble. This truth is recorded in several ways in the Old Testament (i.e. Psalm 75:10) and more than once in the New Testament (i.e. James 4:6). Thus, we understand it to be a broad principle by which God cares for His own. The same word translated "exalt" (NKJV, NASB), or "lift up" (NIV), is used by Mary in her song of praise to God for the privilege of carrying the Christ child when she said, "He has put down the mighty from their thrones and *exalted* the lowly" (Luke 1:52). She references this same broad principle of how God cares for those who make sacrifices for Him and asserts that God has exalted her through the privilege of carrying the Christ child.

While this promise is for all believers, those who serve as elders in the local church need to pay special attention. The responsibility of a servant of God is to obey Him, no matter how hard that is. The encouragement in obedience is that God will exalt the obedient servant—in due time. Just as the repayment for sacrifice in the gospel ministry (Mark 10) is in this life, the reward for humility, this "exaltation" is in this life. Mary was a woman of no significance, who accepted a pregnancy without a husband which put her in the situation of extreme humility, with the potential of hostility from her society. For her willingness to be insulted, gossiped about, and counted as immoral, she was elevated to be "blessed among women" ***in due time***.

Pastors will have many calls for humility through the uniquely challenging circumstances of local church ministry. The humility he must practice is the same as for all believers, namely, strict adherence to God's righteousness even when it results in not coming out on top in the moment. In leadership meetings, a desired change may be rejected by one or more fellow leaders. After preaching his heart out, he may receive a petty criticism from a church member. After repeated calls to a dying member in the hospital, the family may ask some other pastor to speak at the memorial service. When it comes time for a new budget, it may be balanced by not giving him a raise. When he leaves a church and a new pastor comes, the new pastor may be paid substantially more than he was because the church finally realized what was needful.

The central point is this: there will be times when a pastor wants to fight for his rights, to defend his honor, to tell people exactly what he thinks of what he sees in their puny Christianity, but he cannot, because this is how God expects him to act toward fellow believers, "A servant of the Lord must not quarrel but be gentle to all, able to teach, patient, in humility correcting those who are in opposition" (2 Timothy 2:24-25). BUT there is good news at the end of this story. Genuine humility done to honor the Chief Shepherd, brings His exaltation for the believer—in due time. That means that God is going to give encouragement *when He knows it is needed.*

    One of the earliest criticisms in my first church was a judgment that I was not very spiritual because of the way I appeared on the platform. In those days of "pulpit pews" where we waited for our turn to participate in the service, I sat with my legs spread and was informed via my Senior pastor that this critic believed that godly men crossed their legs on the platform. I complied because it was a small thing. Decades later I was in Africa and asked the national partner what I should avoid so as not to offend the pastors I was about to teach. His reply was, "Do not cross your legs when you are sitting on the platform. If you do, they will assume you think yourself to be a big shot." I used this in my teaching of those African pastors. I told them about both instructions, and they, and I, had a good laugh. That exaltation only took 35 years!

    In that same church (my first ministry) we had a man who told me his call from God was to keep the church on the straight and narrow. He was a stickler for following constitutional process. He was ultra-conservative on many things. At one point he criticized me severely to the deacon board over a youth event promotion. He said his piece to the men, and I apologized for what seemed to him as something worldly and offered to change the offending parts of my plan (I will spare you the details) and was sincerely humble. When he shared his concern, he also told the men he and his family might leave the church. After we both spoke, the chairman of the board said, "Thanks for sharing. I think Dave has the right attitude [exaltation]. Do what you have to do, John." *(Meaning if you want to leave, we will not stop you.)*

In another church I received a scorching letter of criticism from a man with whom I did not have a problem. I invited him to lunch and discovered a complete misunderstanding on his part for which I apologized...even though my offending actions came from no ill motive. He was satisfied with that but sometime later he became upset again and wrote another letter. I took it to the Deacons and read it to them. It was the most humiliating and stressful thing I had ever done to that point in ministry. I remember being so stressed that I had a sensation that seemed like I could feel my hair turning gray while sitting there. When I finished, I made myself accountable to the men and said they needed to tell me if I had a blind spot that needed attention. They said they didn't see a problem and they also said, "Do you want us to talk to him?" That was so encouraging.

Besides these leadership challenges, all pastors are called on to be faithful "in season and out." The "good sermon, Pastor" comments after church are a blessing, but what the fruitful pastor longs for is visible growth in his people. He longs for the church to be full and for new programs to be started to train the increasing numbers of disciples. He wants to see people confessing their newfound faith in Christ in the baptismal waters. In short, he longs to see growth in all ways in the work Christ has entrusted to him. Humbling oneself "under the mighty hand of God" means that the fruitful pastor, in conjunction with his congregation, plants the seed of the gospel, waters it, and waits for God to give the increase (1 Corinthians 3:5-6). Sometimes this comes when desired, but often later than the pastor would like.

As a youth pastor I realized that I was just a part of the ministry to my middle and high-school charges. Their parents were the major influence in the equation and the rest of the church ministry also had an impact. By God's grace we saw a few make professions of faith, and some were baptized. Other evidence of walking with Christ came along from time to time. Decades after I left that church, while I was waiting to preach in one of our network churches, a man came in whom I immediately recognized as one of my "kids" from the youth ministry. He was visiting his parents who were part of the church. Later in the day we had a good long catch-up and he said, "You will never know how much you helped me when I was a teenager." Wow, that surprised me because I did not see him as someone who needed much help. Little did I know in those youth ministry years, God was using my simple faithful pastoral work to help this young man choose the narrow path. God exalted my spirit that day. Surely this is what Paul meant when he said to the Christians in Thessalonica, "For what is our hope, or joy, or crown of rejoicing? Is it not even you in the presence of our Lord Jesus Christ at His coming? For you are our glory and joy" (1 Thessalonians 2:19-20).

    The words of Galatians 6:9 flow along this same channel, "And let us not grow weary while doing good, for **in due season** we shall reap if we do not lose heart." Many years after receiving the harsh letters I referred to above, I read another letter sent by the Sheriff I served for 10 years as a volunteer Chaplain director in his organization. Written in response to an inquiry when I was examined for my current ministry role, his words which affirmed my character and helpful ministry brought tears to my eyes. Another very poignant example of this principle came from a church member in my home church. Shortly after I began serving as the pastor, he and his wife left the church without any explanation. Some years later with a new pastor they returned to the church. One time after I preached there, his comment to me was to this effect, "You have grown." Praise the Lord. No doubt I had some rough edges that drove them away, but after 20 years of growing deeper in Christlike character they could see my progress. That encouragement "lifted me up."

There are many examples I could share but I neither want to reveal things in public that belong only to the Lord, nor do I want to appear to be exalting myself. Trust me when I say, I have had many days when I was called on to be humble under God's hand and had to work to stay there. But, if I had walked away from these hard things in vocational ministry, I would never have seen the exaltation God wanted to give me...*when HE knew I needed it.* Faithful service is hard, but God's encouragement fulfills the faithful pastor down deep in his soul. There will be many times when a pastor has to bite his tongue and bide his time because he is absolutely committed to righteousness in his dealings with his people. My encouragement to you, dear reader, is this, "God is not unjust so as to forget your work and the love which you have shown toward His name, in having ministered and in still ministering to the saints" (Hebrews 6:10).

Questions/Ideas for Application

Have you turned down any invitations to ministry either in your community or the broader Christian community? Spend some time remembering why and evaluating your reasoning.

Did you miss an opportunity to grow? Ask God to help you see the next invitation in light of your desire to grow.

Is there a **recent issue** you would have liked to **discuss** with a more experienced mature pastor? Are there long term challenges in your church for which you cannot seem to find solutions?

List the godly men in your life with whom you interact about your life and ministry. Who do you consider to be a mentor or coach? What is the last concern you discussed with them? Are you actively connected with your denomination, association, or faith group? Are you actively cultivating these relationships?

Do you "humble yourself under the mighty hand of God"? (1 Peter 5:6) What does that mean to you? If it is not clear, go back and read the section on humility again.

Do you have examples of times when God exalted you after a humbling episode? Do you thank God when the exaltation comes?

CONCLUSION

This study was born out of the author's deep love for the Lord and His work on earth, the Church. He has designed the local component pieces of the Church to be led by men called elder, bishop, or pastor. These men are key to the effective functioning of the local church. Their success in carrying out Christ's will for His Church is only possible as they consistently grow in Christlike character and pastoral ability. The pastor who is growing will be fruitful as Christ commanded and will accomplish what God desires for him and the church(es) he serves. His consistent growth will also protect him from the ravages of sin both personally and in his impact on the local church.

Growth in life and ministry requires a genuine call from God as affirmed by the Body of Christ. The man thus called must have a full understanding of how spiritual growth is realized and must give himself to the pursuit and practice of those things that enable growth. Both the targets of personal spiritual growth and the path to that growth have been clearly communicated by God in His Word. The fruitful pastor walks on the path of growth for his own sake to honor God and to become better able to teach His people how to do the same.

One of the vital tools God uses to mature every believer is difficulty. The fruitful pastor understands how trials enable growth, and he applies this truth to his life *and* ministry. Because he realizes that God will allow challenging circumstances to direct his growth, he does not run from them nor despair because of them, but he leans on the Lord and stays in the place of training.

The growing pastor realizes that God uses the whole Body of Christ to assist in his growth. Just as the members of the local church need his teaching of God's Word and the guidance of his wise leadership, he needs the input God puts in their heart for him. The fruitful pastor welcomes encouragements and exhortations from others in the Body of Christ because he is consistently listening for God's voice through His people.

Because the fruitful pastor realizes that character is the basis of God-honoring ministry, he works consistently at becoming like Christ. He never takes a day off from the pursuit of godliness. He also gives himself to learning about the unique temptations and challenges of a pastor's position and he works to protect himself and become strong in every way demanded by the role of spiritual leader.

The fruitful shepherd not only seeks to grow as a man of God, but also as a leader of a group of God's people in their pursuit of the godly life and ministry. He realizes that his initial recognition and skill as a pastor must grow if he would effectively lead a growing congregation (both in quality and quantity). He pursues an ever-deepening understanding of God's Word and how to effectively share it with His people so they can grow in Christlike character and in their ability to serve one another. He also gives himself to learn how to lead the flock under his care to do effective ministry.

The path to such growth is first and foremost learned from God's Word. It has been the goal of this study to begin and end with God's plans for His undershepherds. Many books have been written attempting to source wisdom from the leadership knowledge of the world for the pastor. But the fruitful pastor's methodology for ministry must be firmly rooted in God's truth. The godly pastor also realizes that God brings him opportunities to apply the truths of His Word through various ministry engagements. Because of this, the fruitful pastor does not isolate himself but accepts God's invitations to ministry which come through the broader Body of Christ.

I love being a pastor! I love helping people come to know the joy and peace of Christ! I love helping the wandering sheep to get back in step with the Savior. I love seeing Christians in a local church working together to do the mission of Christ! I love hearing the stories of how God has changed lives through the local church near me and in faraway places! I love watching young men take on the mantle of spiritual leadership! I love guiding people to form God-honoring marriages. I love to be in the presence of suffering saints, soon to go home, who are joyfully waiting to enter their heavenly reward! I love the impact of churches working together to help each other be fruitful! I love assisting the men who are leading churches as they work through challenging circumstances!

    I love the life God gave me as He led me in His work! I love the wife he gave me and the children we had together! I love the five ministries God led me to and the experiences He led me into! I love the second godly woman God gave me and the days we have had and will have serving Him in ways yet unknown! I love the Lord for not letting me follow my own path and instead drawing me into this wonderful life of pastoral service!

    I take no glory in any of this but give it all to God. I did not want the life and ministry of a pastor because of what I thought it would be. Instead, what I have received is a rich, meaningful existence empowered by growth as a Christian and as a spiritual leader. I have been blessed to look back and see that the effort I have exerted to know God through His Word, and to live out His truth, has produced a maturity, wisdom, and joy, by the transforming work of the Holy Spirit, which I did not think possible.

    Dear Reader, if I could spend an afternoon with you, I would tell you more of God's blessings and urge you to lean into every aspect of growth as a believer and pastor. Do not waste your time treading water and waiting for something "better" to come along. Pick up God's ways and means of growth and move forward in Him in all the days God gives you.

Appendix "A"
Guidelines for a meaningful meeting with God

Prepare your heart:

- Confess sin, I John 1:9
- This allows full positive fellowship with God
- This allows the Holy Spirit to help you understand scripture
- This allows God to hear your prayers, Psalm 66:18

Look for any/all/one of these as you read the Bible:

God – Who He is, what He is like, what He does

Man – Who we are, what we are like, what we do

Sin – What does God not want us to do

Promise/Principle – what promises does God make; to whom; and what do we learn from God's promises

Command/Choice/Consequence – what commands does God give us; what choices do we face; what consequences will result from those choices

In the Old Testament, try to discern the difference between **timeless principles** which apply to us, and **specific commands** which may have applied only to that Old Testament time period. (1 Corinthians 10)

Go to the Word with your **questions** and prayerfully ask God to help you see answers in the context of principles 1-7

Your interaction with the scripture should result in a **summary statement** that creates an action plan for change in your thoughts and/or behavior. Write down this sentence and **pray it back to God**; write out prayers based on what you've learned

*Lord, thank You...*for whatever you've discovered

*Lord, please help me...*ask Him to help you obey what you've learned

Prayer

Create a **written prayer** list with the following

> Names of all your close family members, leave space to make notes about specific concerns
>
> Names of all co-workers (church or business)
>
> Name of all church members
>
> List of all significant concerning situations

Create a pattern for your prayer time

My plan

- I have a notebook (journal some would call it) where I make a few notes about the day before and I note what my weight is, because that is something on which I am working.

- Then I loosely follow the process outlined above. I choose a book of the Bible and work through it. I note the verse or passage I meditated on and make some notes about what stood out to me and what it means to me today.

- **The prayer section** of the journal has a section for each day.

- Sunday I pray for my duties on that day and any special things about the service. I also pray for my home church and a few other ministries which are in the formative stages

- Monday is my day off and my prayer list is all family and personal needs.

- Tuesday-Friday lists have the people I am responsible for (when I pastored, it was church members, now it is pastors in our network) divided equally over the days

- Each of the Tuesday-Friday lists also has a few of the ministries (then in the church, now in our network) listed and especially the leaders of those ministries.
- I also have a page I call the "hot list" which contains concerns that need daily prayer. For me that includes my wife and our marriage, my physical fitness (after many orthopedic surgeries) pastors with special current needs, our churches without pastors, people I am counseling or mentoring, etc.
- Saturday is a partial day off, so the list is shorter

Appendix "B"
Baptism Ministry Plan

The baptism class covers the basics of baptism and helps people prepare a written testimony.

- We usually have three class sessions

- In session one I introduce the class and requirements (including a hand-out)

- In the second session I give each person 10 invitations with envelopes (custom designed and printed for our church and the date of the service) and ask them to give them to their family and friends.

- We work on the written testimonies in each session. They bring a draft (according to the points I ask them to emphasize) they read the draft, and I use it for teaching and to help them communicate clearly. The written testimony gets the story told clearly both from a doctrinal and personal perspective.

The baptism service

- We have the baptism just before I preach (after the worship section in the middle of the service) and usually I key my message off the experience of last person baptized.

- While the candidate is in the water, I interview them a bit and introduce the person who will read their written testimony. This person is someone they have chosen who has been spiritually significant in their life. After the testimony is read I ask them if they have believed on Christ and then I baptize them. (While I am not opposed to other people participating in the actual baptism, what I have described here is what I did. I do not intend by this to say I think there is only one person in a church who can do the baptizing.)

- I preach a sermon that keys off one or more of the testimonies and is oriented toward the unbeliever and the uncommitted believer.

    I offer this not as the epitome of how to emphasize baptism but as an example of how I have led my churches to make this vital step of faith extremely meaningful to the candidates AND to the congregation and to some guests who need to consider their walk with the Lord.

(I learned this basic approach from Pastor Don Tyler of Brownsburg, Indiana who shared it as part of "Blue Ribbon Committee on Church Growth" conference put on by the General Association of Regular Baptist Churches in about 1989)

BIBLIOGRAPHY

Alcorn, Randy. *Eternal Perspectives Ministries.* October 31, 2024. https://www.epm.org/blog/2018/Oct/12/piper-identifying-fighting-besetting-sins.

Alexander, Joseph Addison. *A Commentary on the Acts of the Apostles.* Liverpool, UK: Banner of Truth Trust, 1857.

Allen, Jason K. *Discerning Your Call To Ministry.* Chicago, IL: Moody Publishers, 2016.

Barclay, William. *The letter to the Hebrews.* Philadelphia: Westminster Press, 1976.

Barna Group. "Why are Pastors Burning out Personally and Collectively." *Barna Access Plus.* March 21, 2023. https://barna.gloo.us/articles/rp-module-1-2.

Brown, Colin. *The New International Dictionary of New Testament Theology.* Edited by Colin Brown. Vol. 1. Grand Rapids, MI: Zondervan, 1975.

—. *The New International Dictionary of New Testament Theology Volume 1.* Edited by Colin Brown. Grand Rapids, MI: Zondervan, 1975.

Brown, Colin, ed. *The New International Dictionary of New Testament Theology Volume 2.* Grand Rapids: Zondervan, 1976.

—. *The New International Dictionary of New Testatment Theology Volume 3.* Edited by Colin Brown. Grand Rapids, MI: Zondervan, 1978.

—. *The New International Dictionary of New Testatment Theology Volume 3.* Edited by Colin Brown. Vol. 3. Grand Rapids, MI: Zondervan, 1978.

Brown, Collin. *The New International Dictionary of New Testament Theology.* Grand Rapids: Zondervan, 1978.

Bruce, F. F. *The Epistle to the Hebrews.* Grand Rapids: Wm B. Eerdmans, 1990.

Buford, Bob. *Drucker & Me.* Brentwood: Worthy Publishing, 2014.

Chapell, R. Kent Hughes & Bryan. *1 & 2 Timothy and Titus.* Wheaton: Good News Publishers, 2000.

Earls, Aaron. "Small Churches Continue to Grow in Number but Not in Size." *lifewayresearch.com.* October 20, 2021. https://research.lifeway.com/2021/10/20/small-churches-continue-growing-but-in-number-not-size/.

Forman, Rowland, Jeff Jones, and Bruce Miller. *The Leadership Baton.* Grand Rapids: Zondervan, 2004.

Chandler, Otis, ed. *Good Reads.* n.d. https://www.goodreads.com/author/quotes/4693730.James_Hudson_Taylor.

Got Questions? Your Questions, Biblical Answers. October 31, 2024. https://www.gotquestions.org/besetting-sins.html.

Gromacki, Dr. Robert. *Stand True to the Charge, An Exposition of 1 Timothy.* Woodlands, TX: Kress Christian Publications, 2002.

Hegg, David W. *Appointed to Preach.* Fearn, Ross-shire, Great Britain: Christian Focus Publications, 1999.

Helm, David. *1 & 2 Peter and Jude.* Wheaton, IL: Crossway Books, 2008.

Hewitt, Thomas. *The Epistle to the Hebrews.* Grand Rapids: Wm B. Erdmans, 1976.

Hiebert, D. Edmond. *Second Peter and Jude.* Greenville, South Carolina: Unusual Publications, 1989.

Jamieson, Bobby. *The Path to Being a Pastor.* Wheaton, IL: Crossway, 2021.

Jefferson, Charles. *The Minister as Shepherd.* Manila: Living Books for All, 1973.

John F. Walvoord & Roy Zuck, Editors. *The Bible Knowledge Commentary.* Wheaton, IL: Victor Books, 1983.

—. *The Bible Knowledge Commentary.* Wheaton, IL: Victor Books, 1983.

Kammell, Craig L. Blomberg and Mariam J. *Exegetical Commentary on the New Testment.* Vol. James. Grand Rapids: Zondervan, 2008.

Keller, Timothy. *Center Church.* Grand Rapids: Zondervan, 2012.

—. *Center Church.* Grand Rapids: Zondervan, 2012.

Kent, Homer A. *The Epistle to the Hebrews.* Grand Rapids: Baker Book House, 1972.

—. *The Pastoral Epistles.* Chicago: Moody Press, 1975.

Lenski, R. C. H. *The Interpretation of St. Peter, St. John, and St. Jude.* Minneapolis, MN: Augsburg, 1966.

—. *The Interpretation of the Epistle to the Hebrews and the Epistle of James.* Minneapolis: Augsburg, 1966.

Lindberg, Christine A., ed. *Oxford College Dictionary.* New York, New York: Putnam and Sons, 2002.

MacArthur, John. *Ephesians.* Chicago: Moody, 1986.

—. *James.* Chicago: Moody, 1998.

—. *Rediscovering Expository Preaching.* Dallas: Word Publishing, 1992.

—. *The MacArthur New Testament Commentary, II Peter & Jude.* Chicago, IL: Moody, 2005.

MacDonald, Gordon. "When Leaders Implode." *Leadership Journal Newsletter*, November 2006: 4.

Mantey, Dan &. *A manual Grammar of the Greek New Testament.* Toronto: MacMillan, 1955.

McKenzie, Michael. *Don't Blow Up Your Ministry.* Downers Grove, IL: Intervarsity Press, 2021.

Milligan, J.H. Moulton AND G. *Vocabulary of the Greek Testament.* Peabody, PA: Hendrickson, 1997.

Mohler, Albert. "Albert Mohler." *albertmohler.com.* August 10, 2018. https://albertmohler.com/2018/08/10/getting-unhitched-old-testament-andy-stanley-aims-heresy.

Moo, Douglas. *Tyndale New Testment Commentaries.* Vol. James. Downers Grove, IL: Intervarsity, 2015.

Newell, William R. *Hebrews Verse by Verse.* Chicago: Moody Press, 1947.

Ogne, Steve, and Tim Roehl. *Transformissional Coaching.* United States: Missional Challenge Publishing, 2019.

Oxford University Press. *The Oxford American College Dictionary.* New York: Putnam and Sons, 2002.

Peterson, Andree Seu. "A Step Beyond Surrender." *World Magazine*, March 23, 2024: 70.

Philipps, John. *The Pastoral Epistles.* Grand Rapids: Kregal, 2004.

Piper, John. *Brothers, We are Not Professionals.* Nashville: Broadman & Holman, 2002.

—. *Desiring God.* New York: Multnomah, 2011.

Prime, Begg &. *On Being a Pastor.* Chicago: Moody, 2004.

Robertson, A.T. *Word Pictures in the New Testament.* Vol. 6. Nashville: Broadman Press, 1933.

—. *Word Pictures in the New Testament Volume 6.* Nashville: Broadman Press, 1933.

Silva, Ken. *Was Peter Drucker a Christian.* June 11, 2012. https://www.apprising.org/2012/06/11/was-peter-drucker-a-christian-the-spin-versus-the-truth/.

Simeon Trust. *Simeon Trust.* 2024. https://simeontrust.org/.

Smietana, Bob. "religionnews.com." *Religion News Service.* May 7, 2023. https://religionnews.com/2023/05/07/scott-sauls-author-and-nashville-pastor-to-take-leave-of-absence/.

Smith, J.B. *Greek-English Concordance to the New Testament.* Scottdale, PA: Mennonite Publishing House, 1955.

Strong, James. *Strong's Exhustive Concordance/Greek Dictionary of the New Testament.* Cincinatti: Jennings & Graham, 1890.

Summers, Ray. *Essentials of New Testament Greek.* Nashville, Tennessee: Broadman Press, 1950.

Swindoll, Charles. *James, 1 & 2 Peter.* Grand Rapids: Zondervan, 2010.

Tasker, R. V. G. *Tyndale NT Commentaries: The General Epistle of James.* Grand Rapids: Eerdmans, 1975.

Thayer, Joseph Henry. *Thayer's Greek English Lexicon of the New Testatment.* Grand Rapids, Michigan: Zondervan , 1974.

Thomas, Scott, and Tom Wood. *Gospel Coach.* Grand Rapids: Zondervan, 2012 .

Vincent, Lynn. "A Chat with Michael Farris." *World*, November 18, 2023: 72.

Vincent, M. R. *Word Studies in the New Testament Volume 1.* McLean, Virginia: MacDonald Publishing, 1886.

—. *Word Studies in the New Testament Volume 2.* McLean Virginia: Mac Donald Publishing CO, 1886.

Vine, W. E. *Vine's Expository Dictionary of Biblical Words.* Nashville, TN: Thomas Nelson, 1985.

Vogel, Jim. *The Pastor, A Guide for God's Faithful Servant.* Arlington Heights, IL: Regular Baptist Press, 2012.

Wikipedia. October 31, 2024.
https://en.wikipedia.org/wiki/Integrity#cite_note-oxford-1.

Wingfield, Mark. "Opinion." *Baptist News Global.* October 21, 2021. https://baptistnews.com/article/the-one-thing-that-most-predicts-a-pastors-success/.

You Tube: Wired. June 2020.
https://www.bing.com/videos/search?q=how+are+treasury+agents+trained+to+spot+counterfeit+money&docid=608038692499511875&mid=1B6B95F78FC4B5F0A2981B6B95F78FC4B5F0A298&view=detail&FORM=VIRE.

Made in the USA
Columbia, SC
09 January 2025